the secret language of flowers

the secret language of flowers

Shane Connolly

photography by Jan Baldwin

RIZZOLI
NEW YORK

Published in 2004
by Rizzoli International Publications, Inc.
300 Park Avenue South
New York, NY 10010
www.rizzoliusa.com

Text copyright © 2004 Conran Octopus
Photography copyright © 2004 Jan Baldwin
Book design and layout copyright © 2004 Conran
Octopus Limited

Library of Congress Catalog Control Number:
2003098266

ISBN: 0-8478-2605-8

Printed in China

Publishing Director: Lorraine Dickey
Senior Editor: Katey Day
Editor: Sharon Amos
Art Director: Chi Lam
Art Editor: Megan Smith
Stylist: Lesley Dilcock
Production Manager: Angela Couchman

contents

introduction

In 1718 a doubty prototype tourist, Lady Mary Wortley Montagu, encountered a system of coded messages used in Turkish Harems called Selam. She was enthralled and immediately copied it by sending a friend a box full of flowers and other objects with a hidden message contained in the specific symbolism of each. A seed had been sown. About one hundred years later, a book called *Le Language des Fleurs* by Charlotte de la Tour (Louise Cortambert) was published in Paris. It gathered together, for the first time, the symbolic meanings of specific flowers. Some of these came from the original Turkish practice, but many more were the fruits of her own painstaking research into ancient mythology and plant folklore. This new science, known as florigraphy, was immediately popular. In England and America, hundreds of similar books were published between the 1830's and 1880's. Each copied, added to, adapted and even discarded Charlotte de la Tour's initial interpretations to suit each author's knowledge and beliefs, or to accommodate some newly discovered flower.

These authors looked to the East and West, to ancient mythology, religious symbolism and medicinal uses; to assign meanings to flowers. A confusing plethora of interpretations was the result, as symbols could be analysed in many ways – positively, negatively, sacredly, profanely – for each flower. But, despite the confusion, flowers were being used to express and even awaken feelings and emotions at a time when strict etiquette suppressed openness. It also appealed to the sentimentality of the new century. Fashionable floral jewellery immortalised these thoughts in its gold and precious gemstones. Later, the pre-Raphaelite art movement enthusiastically embraced florigraphy. Though sadly not all artists were as fluent in botany as they were in the language of flowers, resulting in further confusion and misinterpretation.

Although hugely popular during the 19th century, the language of flowers narrowly survived the ensuing decades, re-emerging only occasionally. The coronation mantle of Queen Elizabeth II, for example, was embroidered with olive branches and wheat in the hope that her reign would be full of peace and plenty. Since then the delicate nuances of floral symbolism have largely been forgotten. Time, however, is cyclical: we are again in an age where communication is both a driving force and an apparent challenge as we strive to make it faster and easier at the cost of true power and meaning. Looking again at this lost language fills me with awe and respect as the story of each flower reveals its ancient roots. The language of flowers is both eloquent and elegant. Flowers have a voice and it is again time to let them speak.

good news

comfort

good wishes

anticipation

enthusiasm

inspiration

childishness

lightheartedness

maternal love

gratitude

fertility

Expectation, births & beginnings

Moss & campanulas

Moss is an unassuming little plant. In *The Comedy of Errors* Shakespeare dismisses it as 'idle', and to the casual observer it does not seem to be in the same rush as other more decorative plants to grow or to flaunt itself. It gets on with things quietly.

Birds appreciate the softness of moss and often use it, combined with feathers, to add the final luxurious touch to their nests. This affiliation of moss with the nesting instinct of birds is almost certainly the route of the meaning of maternal love attributed to moss in floral dictionaries. There is also a traditional belief that robins place moss on graves in winter. Perhaps this legend came about from the fact that moss is one of the few plants that will survive on a grave during a harsh winter. Who knows? But, whatever the facts, the moss implies respect for the person buried, whether a parent or a child, and it is symbolic of the love that exists between a parent and a child. It can be only speculation, but the meaning given to moss seems appropriate for many reasons, not least because of its primal, soft, blanketing nature.

Campanulas, or bell flowers, on the other hand, have a very clear link with their allocated meaning of gratitude. The Latin name *Campanula* means little bell which is, of course, a reference to the shape of the flowers. The genus includes Canterbury bells (*Campanula medium*), which were named after the town of Canterbury, where they grew in abundance and which also happened to be a centre of pilgrimage. The pilgrims' horses wore similarly shaped horse bells and, since the purpose of many pilgrimages is to give thanks, it isn't difficult to see how the link between bells, campanulas and gratitude evolved.

Moss is so often used in floral art merely as a cover-up or a screen for anything undesirable and unattractive. It makes a refreshing change to use it as an intrinsic part of the decoration, as I have here. Several varieties of campanula are available as small plants in full flower, and I simply placed several pots in a wide bowl that was also deep enough to cover the individual flower-pots. I then 'laced' clumps of moss between the pots to create an abstract pattern. The pattern could easily be more formal or even more abstract. Campanulas come in many colours but white varieties seem to be more closely associated with gratitude than the blue shades, which also symbolize constancy.

Moss and campanulas (Campanula cochleariifolia 'Mini White Wonder')

Soft green moss is used to signify maternal love, while the
delicate white bell flowers of campanulas represent gratitude
– a perfect combination for Mother's Day.

Irises

Irises are named after a Greek goddess whose
symbol was the rainbow. Like the proverbial
pot of gold at the rainbow's end, irises signify
good news or a message.

Irises grow in myriad colours, from the most subtle earthy shades to startling, luminous tones. I prefer them arranged simply with no other type of flower; however, irises were a popular subject of many old still-life paintings and can add a wonderful artistic touch to a mixed arrangement. They need little fuss: just clean water, a sharp knife or pair of scissors, and a tall vase to hold them vertically. (Like most flowers that grow stiffly upright, irises can look uncomfortable arranged horizontally.) Try them massed in bowls to imitate the fullness of a growing plant or use them sparingly, as I have, to look almost oriental.

Iris 'Flamenco', 'Mary Frances' and 'Carnaby'

Rainbows are associated with nice things, like pots of gold or far-off mystical lands in Hollywood musicals. Symbolically their floral namesake – the iris – is equally optimistic.

The Greek goddess Iris was the messenger of the gods, and the rainbow was her pathway between heaven and earth. It signified her presence and was the portent of good news. (Coming as it does at the end of heavy rainfall, a rainbow is usually welcome news in itself anyway.)

In Ancient Egypt irises were carved on temple walls and placed in tombs to help the dead travel to the afterlife. This same association existed in Ancient Greece, where another of Iris's duties was to carry the souls of women and girls along the shimmering highway to paradise. Even in modern-day Greece the flowers are frequently placed on the graves of young girls.

Appropriately then, this many-coloured flower was named after the goddess of the rainbow – or perhaps she was named after it – and their attributes merged seamlessly. Much later irises were embraced as Christian symbols: in paintings of the Virgin and Child, they signify the good news of Christ's birth. On a practical level, dried iris root (orris root) was once given to soothe the gums of teething babies. For a mother, this was probably the best news of all.

Put a smile on someone's face with golden buttercups, which represent cheerfulness and childishness, and add a dash of lightheartedness with a spoonful of shamrocks.

Being an Irishman, I have a soft spot for shamrocks. In Ireland, sprigs are sold in every florist shop and greengrocers on St Patrick's Day. By keeping them in water or growing them in a little pot, you can enjoy their infectious lightheartedness a while longer. For both plants you need a dainty jug or pot to really show them off. This old china soup ladle holds just the right amount of water for the shamrocks and makes a charming vase. The jug is equally perfect for a handful of buttercups. *Buttercups* (Ranunculus acris) *and shamrocks* (Trifolium dubium)

Buttercups & shamrocks

Childhood memories invariably include buttercups and the game that tests your fondness for butter by holding a flower under the chin. Just a bit of fun seems to sum up the buttercup's place in the language of flowers – not a flower to be taken seriously. But its regular appearances in medieval church woodcarvings seem to suggest otherwise, as the Church was not known for mirth or jollity. Perhaps the buttercup's golden petals once symbolized the riches of heaven, too.

In the range of flower remedies developed by Dr Edward Bach in the early twentieth century, buttercups are recommended for cases of self-doubt as the flowers' golden warmth can cheer from within and make life seem special again.

Shamrocks can only add to these pleasures. They are a member of the large clover family and associated with good luck. Shamrocks are also the best-known symbol of Ireland, going hand-in-glove with the perpetual image of an Irishman's easy-going joviality, which sometimes verges on parody. The sixteenth-century herbalist John Gerard claimed that shamrocks even have life-saving potential as they stand up and tremble before a severe storm. Now that just has to be a piece of old blarney.

Give the anxious mother-to-be a cool green floral message with gooseberries for anticipation, oregano for birth, bells of Ireland for luck, thyme for strength and courage, and sage to wish her health and a long life.

Gooseberries, oregano, bells of Ireland, thyme & sage

These herbs were essential medicines in the lives of our forefathers, their floral meanings hinting at these roles. Sage was the herbal aspirin of the ancient world and its Latin name – *Salvia*, from the Latin *salvere*, meaning to save – tells us something of its value. Ancient Romans and Greeks used sage to stimulate the memory. Current research shows that it might prove useful in the treatment of Alzheimer's disease.

The Greek word for thyme is *thumon*, which is similar to *Thumos*, a Roman spirit and giver of courage and force. His symbol was thyme, and centurions are known to have bathed in thyme water before battle.

Oregano, known as dittany in floral dictionaries, was another valuable medicinal herb and the mainstay of an army doctor's bag during battle, when it was used as a disinfectant. It would also have been useful during confinement.

Bells of Ireland are, of course, as green as the Emerald Isle and obviously thought to share the proverbial luck of the Irish. Tart green gooseberries make the mouth water in anticipation. And let's not forget the charming story that babies can found under gooseberry bushes.

In the twenty-first century herbs are popular once again and are widely available as growing plants or in bunches of cut stems for cooking. I have mixed a few bunches here with some other ingredients to produce a restful foliage-based arrangement that could also have been made into a generous tied posy. Any one of the herbs with another flower or fruit would make an equally thoughtful, but simpler, arrangement. Leave the herbs still bound in bunches when you make an arrangement like this to produce a relaxed 'wild' effect, which would be lost if the ingredients were mixed together.

*Gooseberries (*Ribes uva-crispa), *oregano (*Origanum vulgare 'Country Cream'), *thyme (*Thymus vulgaris), *sage (*Salvia officinalis 'Purpurascens') *and bells of Ireland (*Molucella laevis)

Red geraniums, basil & forsythia

Forsythia is a flamboyant spring-flowering shrub that epitomizes our anticipation of garden glories to come. For that alone its meaning of expectation would be apt, but it is also named after William Forsyth, director of the Chelsea Physic Garden from 1770, who is remembered for a scandalous controversy involving monumental expectations. He claimed to have invented an ointment that would heal diseased trees and sold the formulation to the British Royal Navy for a vast sum of money. Forsyth had convinced the Navy that his invention would help solve the shortage of ships, which was due to a deficit of large healthy trees for timber to build them. But an expert discovered 'Forsyth's Plaister', as the mixture had been patented, to be no more than ash, soapsuds, lime, cow-dung and urine. Forsyth's supporters evaporated and Forsyth died in 1804 before the matter was settled.

The bright red geraniums that we see in window-boxes throughout Europe were just as popular in the nineteenth century as part of colourful bedding schemes. A native of South Africa, this type of geranium was actually renamed *Pelargonium* in 1787 but we have been a little slow to adopt its new name. Whatever their name, red geraniums will certainly remind you of home and the relative comforts thereof, hence the link between the plant and comfort.

Basil has a long and varied past. To the Romans it was a symbol of love and fertility. Tradition held that if a girl could get a man to accept a basil plant, he would marry her (a pot on her window-sill would attract him in the first place). In Ancient Greece basil was stamped on to avoid bad luck, in Tudor England it was a favourite parting gift to guests, while in India, where it originates, it is a sacred plant and used to cleanse Hindu temples. It has also been used to dispel headaches, menstrual pains and flies. A lucky plant indeed.

Seasonal flowers for an expectant mother: in spring, forsythia symbolizes expectation or anticipation; in summer, red geraniums wish her comfort, with basil to represent good luck.

These are both sweet and simple arrangements that could easily be given as small tied bunches instead. Much of their charm lies in the appropriateness of the meanings and the daintiness of the containers. I always look out for interesting containers to give with flowers as gifts. Forsythia is a large showy shrub but small cut-off sideshoots can look delicate and delightful. That's what I have used here, arranged in an old painted tin pot. It would make a great choice for a baby-shower party or to give to someone awaiting exam results. Likewise the geranium and basil. Geraniums can be a bit demanding on the eye in all the glory of a municipal park display. Cut a few flowering stems, however, and mix them judiciously in a pretty coloured vase with something like these dark sprays of basil to tone things down slightly, and you have a real winner.

Above left: Red geraniums (Pelargonium 'Caligula') and purple basil (Ocimum basilicum 'Purpureum')
Above: Forsythia (Forsythia x intermedia)

Hollyhocks

In the symbolic language of flowers fertility, or more accurately fecundity, is represented by tall stately hollyhocks, in recognition of their embarrassingly prolific procreative habits.

Hollyhocks are members of the ancient mallow family, known and grown since time immemorial. Withered mallow flowers have been found in the grave of a Neanderthal man and in the tombs of Egyptian pharaohs. They apparently grew in the underworld garden of the goddess Hecate, who was a skilled healer. The botanical name for the genus is *Alcea*, from the Greek word for healing, and mallows were used medicinally for centuries, recommended for everything from whooping cough in humans to swollen hocks in horses. Curing the latter was a special attribute of hollyhock leaves, which gave the plant the 'hock' in its name. Holly, or holy, came about because the plants were introduced to the West by the Holy Crusaders.

By the eighteenth century, hollyhocks were extremely popular garden flowers, with increasingly decorative strains, some with double flowers, introduced from China.

As each flower fades, it is replaced by a circular seedhead containing literally hundreds of seeds arranged in a neat radiating pattern. Most of these seeds seem to germinate, whatever the soil and conditions they find themselves in, and gradually spread far beyond their original boundary. They are indeed fertile and generous plants.

It's as well to remember that fertility, or fecundity, can also describe intellectual productivity and resourcefulness, as well as prolific reproduction. So hollyhocks need not frighten off those who would prefer to keep their own procreative habits under strict control!

Hollyhocks make impressive arrangements but they do have a tendency to wilt. You can help prevent this by putting them into water immediately after cutting or, if you buy them, transporting them in water. Putting the bottom 2 cm (1 in) into boiling water for a few minutes can sometimes revive a flagging stem.

It would be a pity to cut these top-heavy flowers into shorter lengths, so you need either a very tall vase or a deep bowl, plus a generous amount of scrunched-up chicken wire to support the stems. I used chicken wire in this arrangement, and the result is as natural and generous as the flowers themselves.

Hollyhocks (Alcea rosea)

Angelica & grasses

Creativity requires inspiration, and this is represented by the lofty herb angelica. Success needs not only industry but also perseverance, and these hardworking qualities are denoted by humble grasses. A good combination to toast a new enterprise or beginning.

Several legends aim to explain how the herb angelica acquired its celestial name. The most devout of these recounts how an angel (in some versions upgraded to an archangel) appeared to a monk during the Great Plague of the seventeenth century. He revealed angelica's valuable healing properties to the monk, advising him to keep its seeds in his mouth to ward off the pestilence. History has not recorded whether this remedy worked, but angelica was certainly used widely in medicine long before and after the plague, and for a surprisingly wide range of afflictions. Gerard, the sixteenth-century herbalist, even claimed that it could cure the bites of snakes or mad dogs. The seeds and roots were also burnt to disinfect houses and to protect against evil spirits – a truly inspirational range of uses.

A second legend claims that the plant is so named because it miraculously flowers each year on the feast of St Michael the Archangel – an assertion that seems excessively inspired and is yet to be proved. Finally, in the northern Baltic countries, where angelica is thought to originate, people say that the plant is named after the northern Russian port of Archangel. Sadly, this least visionary of explanations is probably the most plausible of all.

Sometimes angelica was also referred to as the Root of the Holy Ghost, for reasons that are now obscure. The Holy Ghost was seen as the bringer of inspiration to the first Christians, and this is more likely the real origin of its meaning in the language of flowers. Apparently angelica is popular today among white witches as a giver of energy, vision and inspiration.

Grasses are the world's most persevering plants. Their acquired meaning could not be more apposite as they grow back time and time again, however severe the setback – whether because of drought or over-enthusiastic mowers. Grasses make an unassuming model and inspiration for every new venture and are the perfect symbolic partner for the more ornamental angelica.

Angelica and grasses combined have the divinely tall, wild, unpretentious look associated with the world's most elegant women. An arrangement like this in one of their homes would mean 'I have nothing to prove'. Its look is timeless and its price literally incalculable. It says 'who needs flowers?' and that's something only those who could afford any amount can say. Try these lofty green beauties in tall coloured-glass vases set on the floor and enjoy the towering height of the angelica and wispy wilfulness of the grasses. Many cut ornamental grasses are available to buy and they all make wonderful decorations, as do bamboos and tall branches. Flowers with similar meanings include the stately fennel (strength) and hollyhock (fecundity, see page 23).

Angelica (Angelica archangelica) *and mixed ornamental grasses*

modesty

innocence

purity

constancy

simplicity

naivety

first love

bashfulness

Innocence, simplicity & youth

Lilies symbolize purity and innocence, and also have strong spiritual associations. They are the perfect choice when simplicity is the keynote.

Madonna lilies were the only variety available to medieval artists but, during the past two centuries, many different species and varieties have been discovered and bred. They now come in a bewildering range of types and colours. This has – thankfully – removed most of their associations with death, which largely began because their scent was so 'useful' where corpses were concerned. Lilies look wonderful in most styles of arrangement, either alone or mixed with other flowers. I still relish the sight and scent of Madonna lilies in tall classical vases – characteristically pure and simple.

Madonna lilies (Lilium candidum)

Lilies

Before the era of the Dutch still-life, no artist had ventured to portray the lily in anything less than a sacred environment. Lilies had long been adopted by the Church and were promoted enthusiastically as an emblem of the Virgin Mary's supreme purity.

The Greeks had established the lily's divine links centuries before, however, with the legend that they had first grown from drops of milk spilt from the breast of the mother-goddess, Hera. Juno, Hera's Roman equivalent, had exactly the same story told of her – the Romans even called the lily *Rosa Junonis*, or Juno's rose. Aphrodite, the Roman goddess of love associated with real roses, was said to find the lilies' cold perfection so unappealing that she amused herself by giving them their rather phallic stigmas.

By the Middle Ages the mother of the gods had been firmly replaced by the Virgin Mary, and the lily was used to illustrate her virtues. Its luminous white exterior was flushed with gold inside, like the warmth that co-exists with the Virgin's purity; its scent, like her virtue, could neither be replicated nor eliminated. Lilies thereafter appeared in most images of Mary and, with or without her, will always be associated with simplicity and purity.

Red rosebuds represent the young, pure and lovely, sweet Williams are willing to please and strawberries symbolize perfect goodness – the ideal child.

If you do not already grow wild strawberries, or *fraises des bois*, to give them their posh name, then I suggest you plant some immediately. They are not the ancestor of the humungous strawberries sold in shops today but a different species. The taste is completely different, too, and unforgettably delicious – except apparently to birds, which uncharacteristically leave all the fruit for you.

Wild strawberries are enthusiastic plants, both in fruiting and reproducing, so you will soon be able to cut stems to add to decorations. Here they give an old-fashioned painterly air to a jug of sweet Williams and rosebuds, and make the ordinary truly special.

Sweet Williams (Dianthus barbatus)*, red rosebuds* (Rosa moyessii) *and wild strawberries* (Fragaria vesca)

Sweet Williams, red rosebuds & wild strawberries

Who was the original sweet William? No one can provide a convincing answer, and various Williams, from Shakespeare to the Conquerer, have been suggested. In the sixteenth century, the herbalist Gerard summed up sweet Williams perfectly: 'Not used either in meat or medicine, but esteemed for their beauty to decke up gardens, the bosomes of the beautiful, garlands and crownes for pleasure' – making them a flower truly willing to please.

Rosebuds are given meanings that are charming diminutive versions of their full-blown counterparts. Open red roses represent ardent love and adult beauty; red rosebuds add a hitherto unmentioned youth and purity to the equation.

Wild strawberries have been held sacred since the time of the Romans. The poet Ovid described them as the fruits of Elysium, and Christianity later concurred. Their trifoliate leaves were linked to the Holy Trinity, and the sun-ripened fruits were said to symbolize the fruits of good deeds and spiritual growth. A tea made from their leaves will apparently protect against witchcraft and magic – perfect goodness indeed.

Bluebells & silverweed

Carpeting the woodlands each spring, bluebells symbolize constancy and humility. The silken foliage of silverleaf adds naivety – together they are simplicity and innocence personified.

Until quite recently the botanical name for bluebell was *Endymion*. In Greek mythology, a comely shepherd boy of that name was espied by Selene, the moon goddess, as he slept under the stars. She fell immediately and passionately in love with him and, rather selfishly, conspired to keep him asleep so that she could enjoy his beauty in perpetuity. A woodland carpeted with bluebells has something of Selene's twilight glow about it, and the constancy of her love and Endymion's slumber gave bluebells their meaning, too. His career as a shepherd, though cut tragically short, adds the humble dimension.

The bluebell's new botanical name is *Hyacinthoides*, as it is a member of the hyacinth family, which has its own surprisingly similar tale of lecherous gods, fair mortals and everlasting love (see page 121).

Bluebell roots were once used to make glue and also, according to the herbalist Gerard, to retard the growth of unwanted hair – two applications with long-lasting effects but, hopefully, different concoctions.

Naivety – an endearing, simple-minded innocence – is perfectly characterised by silverleaf. It repeatedly grows on hard soil in gateways and on footpaths and is predictably trodden underfoot. Its pretty leaves were once thought to soothe tired feet when placed inside shoes, resulting in its common name of traveller's ease.

When arranging bluebells the guiding principle is simplicity, which is reflected in the bottle vases I have chosen here. Thinking of the flowers' meanings, I used modest quantities and produced an arrangement of unexpected lightness and magic, as if I had shrunk and become bluebell-sized. Immersing the silverweed in the water in the bottles emphasizes the leaves' silkiness and also makes the long stems of the bluebells seem less naked. Please remember that it is illegal to pick bluebells in the wild, but they are well worth growing yourself from reliably sourced bulbs. If you put the cut ends into a few centimetres of boiling water before arranging them, the flowers will last really well.
Bluebells (Hyacinthoides non-scripta *syn.* Endymion non-scripta) *and silverleaf* (Potentilla anserina)

Most people are very fond of the simple daisy. The name is old English, a charming contraction of 'day's eye', which describes the flower's habit of opening and shutting with the rising and setting of the sun. The same wild daisies (*Bellis perennis*, or the perennial beauty) were associated with various goddesses of love throughout antiquity. By the fifteenth century they had became known as *flos Amore*, or love's flower, and were worn by knights to indicate that their love was returned by their chosen lady. The analogous game of pulling off daisy petals one by one to reveal whether a lover 'loves me' or 'loves me not' probably began much earlier, and games like this, and the making of daisy chains, gradually gave the flowers a stronger affiliation with children and enhanced their association with simplicity. In an odd but natural progression of sorts, the love goddesses were replaced by the Virgin Mary, and the lovers' daisy changed her ways to become purer and more innocent.

Roses, in all colours, combinations and stages of growth, have a wealth of different meanings. In general they signify love, with a rose for every emotion and stage in the affair. These white rosebuds begin the sequence and signify a young girl who is still innocent, or even ignorant, of love. This association is beautifully symbolized by the unopened bud – a metaphor for a virginal girl. An open white rose carries the sentiment 'I am worthy of you'; while a full-blown bloom says 'you are beautiful' – all sentiments for the older girl on the path to love and romance.

Daisies & white rosebuds

Daisies represent innocence and simplicity, while unopened white rosebuds are symbolic of girlhood or those who are innocent of love – the perfect posy for a young bridesmaid.

Roses are excellent in tied arrangements. If a posy is to be held throughout a wedding, make sure that the flowers are well conditioned, keeping them in water until the last moment.

Not all types of daisy make long-lasting cut flowers. Leucanthemums (which include ox-eye daisies and Shasta daisies) last well, although their scent often demonstrates why they are also known as dog daisies. Other daisy-like flowers include members of the aster family and feverfews, but be wary if using them symbolically: feverfew (*Tanacetum parthenium*), the herbal cure-all of the ancient world, represents protection but Michaelmas daisies symbolize a farewell. The marguerites used here are readily available as flowering plants and can be used for very long-lasting displays massed in bowls and watered regularly.

*Marguerites (*Argyranthemum frutescens*) and white rosebuds (*Rosa 'Pandora'*)*

Paeonia

In all their shades of blushing pinks,
peonies are associated with bashfulness.

Peonies

If ever a flower had roots stretching back to ancient times, it is the peony, named in honour of the Greek gods' personal physician, Paeon. He was said to have cured Plato, the god of the underworld, using its seeds. The healing powers of the plant are unproven but it was credited as a cure for 20 different ills by the Roman historian and naturalist Pliny the Elder before he was killed in the eruption of Vesuvius in 79AD.

In the eighteenth century peony roots were worn by children to guard against epilepsy and nightmares, which were both associated with the powers of the underworld. This treatment may explain the origin of the peony's link with childhood.

The use of the flower to represent bashfulness and blushes is not only — though perhaps most obviously — due to its mainly pink colourings. It is reinforced by several other interesting associations. In medicinal usage in medieval times, the peony was thought to have a masculine and feminine form. These were in fact two different species of peony: *P. mascula,* which has a long tapering root, and *P. officinalis* with its feminine feathery leaves. (Later on in Victorian times, such blatant anatomical comparisons would be the cause of many blushes.)

At about the same time Christianity, keen to provide suitable replacements for pagan practices, quickly saw a comparison between the peony and the Virgin Mary — 'a rose without thorns', which the peony appears to be. Virginal modesty and, one presumes, blushes, are another clear association.

In the latter half of the eighteenth century the first tree peony (*P. suffruticosa*) arrived in England from China, where it had always been revered and was traditionally used in poetry to describe the blushes of a young girl. By this time, however, the peony had few medicinal uses but it had retained its popularity, appearing both in the decorative garden and in still-life paintings. In the craze for all things Chinese, these associations were eagerly adopted, adding to and reinforcing existing traditions.

Although this beautiful flower eventually came to represent bashfulness, according to some flower dictionaries the peony is also symbolic of devotion, both religious and matrimonial, presumably because of its early affiliation with the Virgin Mary.

Peonies are beautiful at every stage. Arrange them simply, as here, in a jug of fresh water and enjoy watching the petals unfurl. Remove a proportion of their leaves, especially those below water level. This seems to help the stems drink enough water to supply the large flower heads. A wilting flower can often be revived if all competing foliage is removed and the stem is re-cut and placed in warm water. Peonies are also happy to be arranged in floral foam, provided they have been given a long drink in fresh water beforehand. Always re-cut the stem before arranging the flower. When the flowers are fully open, they can become a bit top-heavy, so cut them short and rearrange them, massed voluptuously in low bowls.

Flowers with similar messages include violets (modesty, see page 43), marjoram (blushes, see page 65) and deep red roses (bashful shame).

Right: Peonies (Paeonia lactiflora *'Sarah Bernhardt')*
Previous pages, from left: Peonies (Paeonia lactiflora *'Cornelia Shaylor',* P. officinalis *'China Rose',* P. officinalis *'Rubra Plena',* P. lactiflora *'Cornelia Shaylor',* P. lactiflora *'Magic Orb' and* P. officinalis *'Rubra Plena')*

Sweet violets are linked with a delightful trio of old-fashioned virtues:
innocence, modesty and decency.

Violets

Once upon a time there was a beautiful girl named Io. In ancient times, great beauty was not necessarily a blessing as it often seemed to attract the unsolicited attentions of one of the gods or goddesses. In this case, Io captivated Zeus himself. Unfortunately for her, Zeus's wife, Hera, was very jealous and challenged the excessive attentions he was paying the girl. Zeus denied all charges but, to ensure continuing domestic harmony, conceived a cunning plan. He would turn Io into a white heifer and, as compensation, give her a field of delicious purple violets to eat. The Latin *Viola* descretly honours her name.

When Hera saw this irresistible little creature in her field of purple flowers, she was still suspicious and resolved to get rid of her once and for all. She sent a vicious gadfly to torment her until, in desperation, Io threw herself into the sea (which has ever since been known as the Ionian sea in a further attempt to make amends for the indignities she had suffered). After all this, it's hardly surprising that Hera successfully persuaded Io to vow that she would never see Zeus again; in return, Hera turned her back into a woman.

And so it was that violets came to be linked with love that was, albeit unintentionally, innocent and unspoilt. They also represent decency as that was, after all, the motivation behind Zeus's misguided handling of the whole affair.

Violets continued to be highly desirable flowers and, by the Middle Ages, had come to be associated with the Virgin Mary. The plant's unusual method of reproduction seems to support this link. The purple flowers that we see in spring are infertile; the plant actually sets seed later in the year from unprepossessing flowers that bow modestly downwards and are self-pollinating. This made, of course, a perfect physical analogy for the Immaculate Conception. The symbolism stuck and from then onwards violets were grown in every monastery and convent garden in honour of Mary and as a reminder that modesty, innocence and decency are ideal virtues.

As cut flowers go, the life expectancy of violets is relatively short, but don't let that put you off. Violets are inexpensive and sending a loved one a generous bunch tied with velvet ribbon or enclosed in a tissue-lined box is a magical and unforgettable gesture and an increasingly rare treat today. If you are given violets, arrange them simply in bowls of water. Keep them in their tied bunches as the flowers are too delicate to deal with individually. Spraying them with a fine mist of water prolongs their life, while complete immersion overnight in a bowl of water revives flagging stems.

Flowers with similar meanings include daisies (simplicity and innocence, see page 37) and white lilies (purity, see page 30).

Sweet violets (Viola odorata)

Primroses & purple lilac

Like the heady scent of lilac and primroses, there is something intoxicating about youthful romance. These two flowers, individually or combined, perfectly symbolize the innocence, emotions and hope of those first amorous infatuations.

Primroses are literally the *prima rosa*, the first rose of the year, and roses are the flowers most associated with love in all its manifestations. Even their generic name *Primula*, 'little first one', seems distinctly warm-hearted and juvenile when you discover it in the mature formality of a botanical dictionary. It seems rather a shame to introduce the species name *vulgaris* into the middle of all this loving tenderness but primroses were – and still are – commonplace in many country areas in spring. A charming old superstition says that if a maiden encounters a bank of primroses flowering before Easter, she will be married by Christmas.

Over the centuries poets have associated this little flower with modesty, youth and young love. In *Hamlet* Shakespeare whimsically called these first stirrings the 'primrose path of dalliance'.

Lilacs originated in Persia and arrived in France, the land of eternal romance, via Constantinople. The eighteenth-century Swedish botanist Linnaeus gave them the generic name of *Syringa*, which comes from the Greek word for pipe or flute, probably because the stems can be hollowed out. But with France and romance in the equation, you could adopt the more fanciful notion that it was because the flowers are shaped like champagne flutes.

Pure white lilac flowers are used to symbolize memories of youth (see page 141), but purple lilac, perhaps because of its somewhat more sensual colouring, is allied to first love and all its accompanying faltering emotions. Lilac plants are extremely long-lived, rather like enduring memories of happy days and young love.

Primroses represent early youth and young love, while heady purple lilac symbolizes first love or the first emotions of love. Together they make a tender and sweetly nostalgic twosome.

There is nothing more heart-warming than a bank of primroses in spring, but they must never be cut from the wild. Instead, buy primrose plants from a reliable cultivated source and give them to a past love. Or plant them yourself in memory of previous loves, so that you can reflect and dream again each spring. Primroses look delightful arranged in small pots indoors for a while before planting out, or popped into baskets surrounded by moss or pebbles. Here, primrose flowers picked from the garden make a perfect posy surrounded by their own leaves, just as they are when growing naturally.

For the specific treatment of lilacs, see page 141, but, in any case, it is important to remove most of the foliage from branches cut from the garden if they are to last well. I like to use garden lilac in liberal quantities, arranged wildly and artlessly in vases of water.

Primroses (Primula vulgaris) and purple lilac (Syringa vulgaris)

affection

captivation

rapture

caution

solicitude

consideration

thoughtfulness

sentimentality

fondness

constancy

cordiality

Fun, frolics

& friendship

Ranunculus

The messages of 'you are radiant with charms' and
'rich in attractions' are smoothly conveyed by ranunculus.
Boost a friend's flagging ego with these flattering thoughts.

In the 1660s a traveller named Sir John Chardin toured the legendary paradise gardens of Persia and was captivated. One of the flowers he saw there seemed to be a form of the native English buttercup (*Ranunculus acris*) but in a dazzling array of different colours that completely charmed him. Reasoning that a near relative would enjoy moving to an environment where its cousin flourished in every field, he arranged to have some of the plants packed up and shipped back to England. Ranunculus are part of a group of plants that do indeed include the buttercup, and they were an immediate success.

Their arrival in England coincided with the start of the flower societies that were soon to sweep the country in the quest for variety, competitive perfection and general good gardening entertainment. The new ranunculus was seized upon with enthusiasm and, by the start of the eighteenth century was already being widely bred and hybridized just forty-odd years after its discovery.

By the end of the century there were more than eight hundred varieties of ranunculus. It had almost become the tulip of its day, so huge was its popularity and so great the quest for new, ever more exciting varieties. Little wonder then that it was accorded meanings that suited its popular cult status: rich and various in attractions, radiant with charms. It had become the pop icon of a pop-less world and everyone wanted to know and grow this flower.

The epilogue to this tale is not such a happy one. The Persian ranunculus really preferred its original home and, having been bred and interbred, became sickly and developed an unfortunate reputation for being difficult to grow. The plants had fallen from grace by the end of the nineteenth century; a place in the flower dictionaries was the only remaining hint of their former glory.

Ranunculus have regained some of their former cult status in recent years, particularly as a cut flower. Developments in greenhouse growing techniques have meant that the difficult varieties can be catered for and new and better cutting varieties developed.

They are a relatively long-lasting flower but prefer to be arranged in water rather than floral foam. The main problem with ranunculus is that the stem becomes rotten and the heavy heads snap off. To avoid this, remove as much foliage as possible and arrange the flowers in a container that supports the heads. I have massed these flowers in a deep bowl where they can lean on the rim and on each other.

Other flowers to boost the ego include striped roses ('you are full of variety'), short-stemmed sunflowers ('I admire you') and peach blossom ('your charms are unequalled').

Mixed ranunculus (Ranunculus asiaticus)

Show your support for an artistic friend with auriculas – the floral symbol of
artists and painting – and the evergreen foliage of box, which suggests constancy
and devotion in friendship and stoicism in the face of disappointment.

Auriculas & box

The Romans were probably the first to discover that box foliage could be trimmed and clipped to form rigidly sculptural shapes. They called the art form *opus tonsillia*, or barber's work. By 1592 this type of intensive foliage sculpture was called topiary and was all the rage. Box plants seem oblivious to these constant cutbacks and simply respond with persistent healthy growth. This tenacious attitude, coupled with its luscious evergreen leaves, earned box its links with devoted friendship and stoicism. Boxwood, being dense and strong, was also highly prized in the art world for carving wood blocks to make prints.

The venerable auricula would have been the subject of many such prints. A new colour or form can still make enthusiasts quiver with excitement. By the latter half of the seventeenth century the cult of the auricula was in full swing. In 1757 the first green flower was bred and soon after came a slate grey one, which, along with the now-vanished striped flower, became the most highly prized of all. The auricula has a range of colours unique in the world of flowers, ranging from red to gold via amethyst and bronze. Artists as well as gardeners appreciated this floral palette and soon auriculas appeared in every still-life painting. And by the nineteenth century the auricula had itself become the appropriate floral symbol of the painter's art.

I find auriculas totally irresistible. At the height of their fame they were exhibited in specially constructed 'theatres', which displayed them, jewel-like, upon tiered shelves with rich velvet backdrops. This is a poor-man's version of those theatres and is much easier to make than it looks. I used a special square of floral foam designed for funeral tributes. These come in many shapes, so be bold and experiment. Cut box foliage is available from florists or you can use hedge trimmings. Insert small sprigs into the foam as closely together as possible but leave empty spaces for the auricula plants. When it is densely covered, trim the box shape tightly like a piece of topiary.

You could try this idea on a larger scale or with other types of containers. Alternative plants are hoya (for sculpture) or reeds (for music).

*Auriculas (*Primula auricula*) and box (*Buxus sempervirens*)*

Pansies & violas

Pansies say 'think of me', while violas, depending upon their colour, represent sentiments of happiness and friendly thoughtfulness.

The wild pansy (*Viola tricolor*) has quite an illustrious past. These unprepossessing flowers have long been thought to posess magical and healing powers, especially in both medical and emotional matters of the heart. This earned it the charming common name of heartsease, and a mention in several of Shakespeare's plays.

At the beginning of the nineteenth century, however, this little weed became very grand indeed after it was crossed with a Turkish and a Crimean relative to produce the pansy as we know it today. It soon became all the rage, and many more elaborate and colourful forms were quickly developed. The name pansy comes from the French *penser*, meaning to think. It was immediately absorbed into the then equally fashionable language of flowers as a symbol of loving thoughts. Despite its ancestor's association with affairs of the heart, the loving thoughts implied were strictly platonic; more often than not, pansies were used to convey affectionate greetings between friends.

An elaborate list of meanings was accorded to violas of different colours so that the complete family became an important part of the floral dictionary. Blue means 'I will always be true and loyal'; purple, 'you are in my thoughts'; yellow, rural happiness; white, modesty and purity.

In Bach flower remedies viola is used to give a boost of energy, and this seems very much an appropriate use for a flower that is so closely associated with loving friendship.

Pansies and violas are most often seen as bedding plants and, as such, can be temporarily enjoyed indoors, growing in a collection of pots. They make difficult cut flowers as their stems are so short. Try floating flower heads in shallow bowls of water, as I have done in this simple arrangement, which allows you to appreciate the full beauty of the flowers. You could also use zinnias to express thoughts of absent friends (see page 145).

Pansies *(Viola x* wittrockiana*) and violas* (V. *x* williamsii*)

Columbines

In spite of their past religious links, nodding columbines have become symbols of folly and caprice – the epitome of carefree fun or foolishness.

There are at least seventy species of this hardy herbaceous flower so beloved of old cottage gardens. They mix well with other late spring flowers and also suit their company in indoor arrangements. But I also love to use columbines alone when their long delicate spurs can be seen without distractions. They are very easy flowers to grow and were traditionally sown in pots to bring indoors in flower – a good idea worth reviving. Arrange them stylishly in sleek single-coloured vases or bring out their fun side – and your own – with quirky containers like these old French tins.

Other flowers to try are larkspur (hilarity and levity) or chrysanthemums (cheerfulness).

Columbines (Aquilegia vulgaris)

The name columbine comes from *columba*, the Latin for dove. If you turn a flower upside down, you can visualize a coterie of five doves drinking at a bowl. True, the long-spurred variety you see opposite looks more like a gaggle of angry geese, but just use your imagination. The similarity was keenly exploited by the Church to associate columbines with the Holy Ghost, who had traditionally been portrayed as a dove. This most complex and Gothic-looking flower appeared increasingly as a symbol of grace and redemption in religious art between the thirteenth and sixteenth centuries.

But how could this flower, with such elevated associations, have come to represent folly in the language of flowers? After the Reformation, religious symbolism was frowned upon and thoughts about the columbine became temporal. The plant's long spurs, which may have given rise to its botanical name of *Aquilegia* (from *aquilegus*, a tall vessel to hold water) also look like horns – the ancient symbol of a cuckold. An adulterous wife would certainly be thought capricious and her husband callously considered foolish. Later, the flower's common name became granny's bonnets, the heavenly dove analogy replaced by the mundane image of bonneted old ladies gossiping in a group. The stellar columbine had fallen to earth.

I love using trails of flowering plants with fruit – they always seem to be compatible. Jasmine is the plant I most often use in this way. Pots of growing jasmine, in full flower, hidden among fruit in bowls create wonderful arrangements that look far more impressive than they deserve to, given the minimum effort involved. You can usually buy this species of jasmine as a pot plant trained around small metal hoops. Carefully untwine the stems before using them in decorations. I stand the pots in a large bowl and gradually add the fruit around and through the trails until the pots are hidden and the whole thing looks good enough to eat, which, of course, it is!

Try jasmine with citrus fruits in winter: oranges symbolize generosity, which combines well with jasmine's amiability.

Pears and jasmine (Jasminum polyanthum)

Pears & jasmine

In an exquisite fifteenth-century painting of the Madonna and child by Carlo Crivelli, the infant Christ holds a pear to symbolize his tenderness and compassion. Pears have been emblems of affection for centuries and were carved into the elaborate ceilings and door surrounds of grand houses to indicate the warmth within. In the country, pear trees were often planted in boundary hedges to avoid ill-will or disputes with neighbours. (But beware, in China the word for 'pear' and 'separation' is the same, so there your message might be misconstrued.)

Jasmine, on the other hand, seems welcome the world over; even to dream about jasmine is considered auspicious, albeit unlikely. The plant originates in India or Arabia and arrived in the West so long ago that no one knows how. Jasmine has always been associated with love in the East, and there are many beautiful stories attached to it. In the West its associations are more prosaic: it was often planted beside outside lavatories, where its sweet smell played an essential role. Love was therefore toned down to become amiability. Friendliness even describes the scent: jasmine oil blends happily with other essential oils to mimic the scent of a different flower (for example, tuberose and jasmine oils combine to produce the scent of hyacinths).

Pears represent affection, and jasmine is symbolic of amiability or friendliness
    – the perfect combination for a dinner with good friends or simply for telling someone
how much you appreciate their warmth and understanding.

Seeing rhubarb used decoratively is almost as rare as having your doctor prescribe it for a tummy upset. Here, I have used some of its flowering shoots along with the more recognizable edible red stems, but the stems are superbly decorative in themselves when seen magnified through the glass carafe. Try using them to completely line a simple glass tank or cylinder, and then piling it high with gloriously clashing roses or dahlias. Rhubarb has many possibilities symbolically and aesthetically. It behaves well as a cut flower, although the water quickly develops the scent of rhubarb pie.

Rhododendrons make great cut blooms, either in large branches or as short-stemmed handfuls of flower heads. Three generous flower heads make this simple arrangement, with the golden glass vase contrasting beautifully with the colours of the blooms.

*Rhubarb (*Rheum x hybridum*) and rhododendrons (*Rhododendron *'Percy Wiseman')*

Rhubarb & rhododendrons

Rhubarb symbolizes advice while rhododendrons add gravitas to the message, with warnings of danger and an earnest plea to beware – a subtle way to initiate a conversation about reckless new ventures or ill-fated affairs.

No one appears to have actually eaten rhubarb for nourishment until 1778 when the first recorded rhubarb tart was served. From about that time comes the traditional notion that serving rhubarb pie to a loved one brings them under your control. And to some people, control and advice are inseparable.

Before its debut in a pie, rhubarb had been a prized medicinal herb for at least two thousand years in its native China and Tibet, and later in Persia and Arabia. In the nineteenth century, American pioneering families were still being advised to keep indispensible rhubarb roots in their medicine chests. So it is to rhubarb's medicinal past, rather than to its more recent sweeter persona, that we must look to find links with advice.

Conversely, the rhododendron's connection with danger starts specifically with a sweet tooth. In 400BC Xenophon described how the retreating Greek army was almost wiped out near the Black Sea after a shameless soirée with pillaged local wine and honey. The natives had neglected to warn their thieving visitors that the honey was made from the poisonous pollen of the local rhododendron (R. luteum) and had to be diluted before consumption. There are still a few cases of poisoning every year, so beware eating honey produced near rhododendrons!

This small autumnal arrangement is chic and simple. A handful of deep burgundy dahlias forms the main floral content and deliciously scented black peppermint sprigs complement their colour. Herbs are easy to grow and equally easy to buy, with every supermarket offering a selection of growing or cut herbs for the keen cook. Enjoy them in an arrangement first – with or without flowers. Here the oak leaves have begun to assume their moody autumnal colours and add the finishing touch. A sleek angular vase, keeping the ingredients strongly grouped, gives an unaffected, modern look.

Dahlias (Dahlia *'Night Queen'), peppermint* (Mentha piperita) *and oak* (Quercus frainetto)

Dahlias, peppermint & oak

For the hostess with the mostess: dahlias represent good taste, peppermint depicts warmth and cordiality, and a sprig of oak symbolizes hospitality.

Dahlias were not a great success when the Spanish first brought them to Europe from Mexico. At the Jardin du Roi in Paris, the curator thought them so unattractive that he explored the possibility of eating their tubers as a potato substitute. It was not a success – the Aztecs may have eaten them enthusiastically but Western palates were not impressed. Could this link with good taste be a subtle gibe at an earnest Frenchman's botanical experiment? Perhaps not. The dahlia went on to flower at the Empress Josephine's magnificent gardens at Malmaison at the end of the eighteenth century, and her elegance and good taste were *par excellence*.

Our next ingredient, peppermint, is definitely edible. Peppermint tea is synonymous with the warmth and hospitality of Morocco. When heated the leaves release menthol, which activates our perspiration glands, so the warmth is not just emotional. This quality has long been used to stave off colds and 'flu and to help with digestion – the best hosts still serve mints after dinner.

Oak is associated with strength, courage and bravery, as well as hospitality. An oak tree sheltered and saved the infant Zeus from his psychopathic father, and sprigs of oak welcomed King Charles II on his return to London after the Restoration in 1660.

Periwinkles recall memories of early friendship. Added to this are vine leaves for drunkenness, larch for boldness and, for the inevitable blushes, marjoram.

This casual arrangement should be put together without too much effort if it is to work really well. This is harder than it sounds – you must control the artist within – but the symbolic story is more important. I used an African clay vessel (with a watertight vase of water placed inside) and simply added the ingredients in handfuls. The result: an arrangement that looks wild, natural and artless. A little matching bowl holds some unripe grapes and a single vine leaf.

Periwinkles (Vinca minor), larch (Larix decidua), vine leaves (Vitis vinifera) and marjoram (Origanum vulgare)

Periwinkles, larch, vine leaves & marjoram

In the marriage rhyme 'Something old, something new, something borrowed and something blue', the 'blue' traditionally refers to a periwinkle. It was customary to plant one in the newlyweds' garden to bring them happiness, and a periwinkle flower was often tucked into the bride's garter – perhaps a hint at its more ancient use as an aphrodisiac. Its botanical name, *Vinca*, comes from the Latin *vincire*, to bind – an appropriate symbol of marriage or friendship. Less cheerfully, periwinkle flowers were used in Roman sacrificial rites. Perhaps following on from that, their trailing stems were wound around condemned men in the Middle Ages.

Leaves from a grapevine have an obvious link with wine and drunkenness; audacity and larch also have an interesting affiliation. In the mid-eighteenth century, in a bold and sweeping gesture, the Duke of Atholl created the first-ever forestry plantation of seventeen million larch trees on his Perthshire estate. The link with boldness is also apparent in Bach flower remedies, in which larch is used to give confidence.

And, finally, marjoram and blushes. This probably stems from the notion that a virgin would see her true love if she placed a sprig of marjoram under her pillow on Midsummer's Eve.

unity

harmony

conquest

beauty

fantasy

allure

rapture

desire

ecstasy

fascination

secrecy

Loving, longing & lusting

Cow parsley has a number of common names, including fairy lace, which conjures up visions of fantastical dream worlds. In days when amusements were simpler, the brief yearly transformation of every country lane to fluffy white nirvana gave rise to many children's stories and fairytales. Perversely it was considered unlucky to pick cow parsley in many parts of Britain. Another common name, Queen Anne's lace, might go some way towards explaining this reputation. The name is probably a derivation of Queen Anne's loss, as the unfortunate Queen was pregnant eighteen times between 1683 and 1700 but gave birth to only five living babies. Of those five, just one survived infancy and he, too, died before succeeding to the throne.

Cow parsley & eucharis

Frothy cow parsley represents fantasy and eucharis symbolizes maidenly charms. Combine them to tell someone that their feminine assets are the stuff of dreams.

In Ireland cow parsley was known by yet another name, lady's lace but, fortunately, there are no lamentable associations. It was enthusiastically cut and used to decorate altars in May, in honour of the Virgin Mary, after whom it was named.

Eucharis has a much simpler resumé. In Greek mythology Eucharis was an amiable nymph who attracted the attention of Telemachus, the son of Odysseus. Her name in Greek means agreeable or attractive, and when this flowering bulb was discovered in South America, it was named after this gentle being. The flowers have an elusive and subtle scent that is supremely feminine. This, combined with the plant's chaste white flowers and modest way of tilting its head downwards, gave eucharis its well-deserved meaning of maidenly charms.

Cow parsley is a prolific wildflower but it is always best to ask permission before picking it in the wild. It is sometimes sold in flower shops. Whatever the origin, when you get it home place the freshly cut stems in a few centimetres of boiling water and leave them until the water cools. This process helps the stems to last longer when arranged. Eucharis flowers, as one might expect from a perfect lady, are well behaved and undemanding but their delicate petals are easily bruised so handle them gently. With cow parsley they make an unusual and lovely combination. I would arrange them loosely and daintily, perhaps in tall glass containers, to appreciate fully the translucency of the cow parsley and the refined delicacy of the eucharis.

Cow parsley (Anthriscus sylvestris) *and eucharis* (Eucharis grandiflora)

Stephanotis & gardenia

There is a deceptive coyness in this apparently innocent partnership. It belies the brazen message contained in the language of its virginal white flowers – although their combined scent would be enough to tempt anyone to draw nearer.

Both flowers have been variously associated with travel: either a desire or solicitation to travel, in the case of the stephanotis, or a journey to guaranteed pleasure and ecstasy with the gardenia. Perhaps this is not surprising given that both plants had travelled quite a way from their native South Africa when they were first introduced to the West in the eighteenth century.

The gardenia was discovered by a certain Captain Hutcheson taking an afternoon stroll along a South African beach on the way home from India to England. How extraordinary that first glimpse must have been: even to the initiated, a gardenia in full bloom is a wonderful sight. We can imagine the journey to sensory ecstasy it gave Captain Hutcheson in 1754, and it still excites a wider audience today.

Stephanotis whispers a seductive 'come to me' while the gardenia promises a rather saucy 'transport to ecstasy' – a truly potent pairing.

Both stephanotis and gardenia are most often sold as pot plants. Individual flower heads can also be bought in wholesale flower markets and are used mainly in wedding bouquets and headdresses. Stephanotis plants are usually supplied trained rigidly around a little hoop, which appears sadly unimaginative and restrictive to me. I much prefer to untangle the vine carefully (easier if the flowers are still in bud and so less prone to damage) and place it among bowls of citrus fruits. This way the pot is hidden and the stephanotis convincingly mimics the fruits' glossy leaves and scented blossom. Alternatively, I cut off small sections of the vine and use them as cut flowers, as I have done here. The cut ends need to be split and placed in fresh water rather than floral foam to ensure that the flowers will last happily for several days. The remaining plant will continue to grow and flower again.

A typical gardenia pot plant is somewhat parsimonious with its opulent flowers and can look rather mean sporting a single reluctant beauty hidden by an excess of foliage. In that case it is better to use the plant as a flower producer, rather than an *objet d'art* in its own right, keeping it out of sight and cutting off the bloom to enjoy it in its full solitary glory, as I have done here. Again, I recommend water rather than floral foam and, like the stephanotis, the gardenia plant will live on to produce more flowers.

Stephanotis (Stephanotis floribunda) and a single gardenia flower (Gardenia jasminoides)

Bindweed

Bindweed, that beautiful scourge of all gardeners, lays its off-putting reputation aside and makes a tempting suggestion: 'let us unite'. Use this under-appreciated flower as a novel overture to a romantic proposal – or a raunchy proposition.

Attractive though its flower is, bindweed would not make it onto any gardener's list of favourite plants. It is a pernicious weed and a blatant opportunist. Even a tiny piece can regenerate, grow and, as the herbalist Gerard so rightly put it in the sixteenth century, 'taketh hold upon… whatsoever standeth next unto it'. It really is a nasty piece of work and its common names reflect this: devil's guts, robin-run-the-hedge and snake's meat, to name but a few.

Bindweed is simply a rather pushy member of the convolvulus family, which also includes the highly desirable morning glory. Convolvulus comes from the Latin *convolvere*, meaning to entwine or twist, and this is the characteristic, alluded to by Gerard, that is at the root of its unpopularity. Once the stem has twisted round another plant, it is extremely difficult to convince it to untwist. Interestingly, bindweed always twists in the same direction, irrespective of habitat – anticlockwise as you look at it from above.

Florally speaking bindweed says 'let us unite', and I can't imagine a more appropriate phrase. The union it has in mind, though, seems rather oppressive and strangulating, and possibly quite permanent. In Bach flower remedies one of the uses for bindweed is to help break addictions. A bindweed simply wants to be for ever. I hope that has not put you off your proposal.

I had never thought of using bindweed decoratively before and was thoroughly captivated by the result. Amazingly, the flowers seemed to be equally delighted to be appreciated and lasted for days. But even if they survive only a few hours, they are worth using for their suggestive message and novelty value alone. Get them into water promptly after cutting them. Fairly short stems and no leaves at all seem to be the key to success. Bindweed flowers are surprisingly delicate, given the toughness of the plant, so handle them carefully to avoid rips and bruises. The spiral flower buds are truly exquisite and will also gradually open in water.

Bindweed flowers (Calystegia sepium)

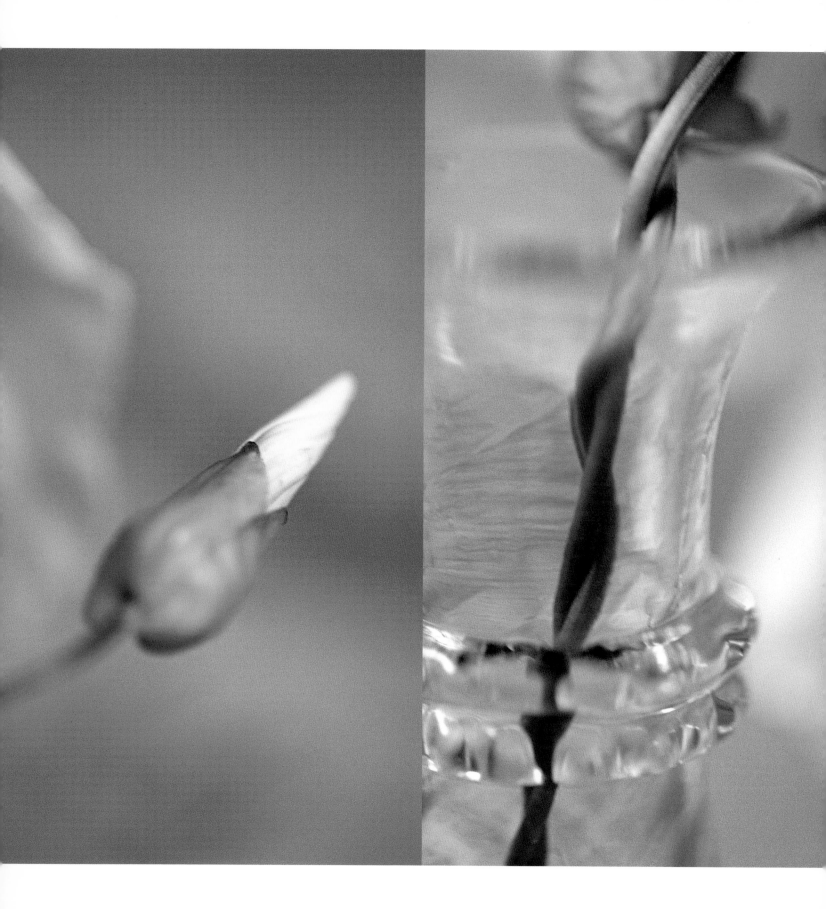

Convolvulus

Calla lilies & ferns

Calla lilies represent feminine beauty or delicacy, and ferns are for fascination. This graceful combination lets a lady know that her womanly charms have been noticed.

The inspiration behind this long-lasting arrangement came from a wonderfully outsized shell that reminded me of the one on which Venus rides the waves in Botticelli's famous painting. I placed small fern plants in the shell (most cut ferns make short-lived foliage, so growing plants are best) and added sections of floral foam between them to hold the calla lily stems. I encouraged some lilies to flow out of the container to show off their long-legged loveliness, and I spread out the fern fronds to cover up the foam.

Send similar charming messages with arrangements of hibiscus flowers (delicate beauty) and dwarf sunflowers (adoration).

Calla, or arum, lilies (Zantedeschia aethiopica 'Crystal Blush') and ferns (Asplenium trichomanes)

The Victorians were ardent collectors of ferns; they built ferneries, dells and stumperies to house them in their gardens, and elaborate glass cases indoors. Between 1840 and 1900, this interest bordered on the obsessive and it is hardly surprising that ferns came to represent fascination in the floral dictionaries concurrently being compiled.

Ancient folklore puts ferns firmly on the list of plants conducive to romance. Traditionally, an unsuspecting man could be enticed by a keen maiden if she baked him a cake containing fern spores that she had harvested in a pewter dish using a hazelwood fork – the touch of a hand would break the spell. Seed gathered in the same way at midnight on Midsummer's Eve could apparently render a person invisible if placed in their shoes – not quite so romantic but useful perhaps.

And, finally, there is the old custom of cutting off a fern frond close to the base of the plant to see the initial of your future spouse appear on the cut stem. Fascinating information in itself and the perfect context for a plant symbolizing romantic fascination.

Originally from South Africa, calla lilies, which are now more usually known as arum lilies, were a popular garden flower in Victorian times. Their graceful form has an undeniably sensual beauty that is distinctly feminine; according to traditional lore, they sprang from the tears of Eve as she left the Garden of Eden.

Rosa

For tender expressions of love – or even longing or lust – roses will help you say a thousand meaningful new things.

Roses

When the tomb of the boy-king Tutankhamun was discovered in the 1920s, one of the most poignant findings was a little bunch of withered roses, placed in the innermost sarcophagus by his young widow thousands of years before. What is most remarkable is that, while Egyptologists can only speculate about many aspects of that ancient burial, the symbolism of the roses is still completely fresh and potent.

Roses have always been associated with the many facets of love, desire and beauty: they were supposedly created by the jealous Roman goddess of nature, Cybele, in an attempt to rival Venus's beauty. Rumour has it that Cleopatra had her pillows stuffed with fresh rose petals every evening, while the Romans associated roses with the passion and excess of their orgies (see page 146). Roses have also been linked to Brahma, Buddha, Vishnu and Confucius, and the Christian Church finally adopted them as a symbol of chaste, celestial love. Roses became the special flower of the Virgin Mary, just as they had been dedicated to the Greek goddess of love, Aphrodite, many centuries before.

The Church's embrace was responsible in many ways for bringing more rose species to the West. Hybridization reached a peak in the nineteenth century when the language of flowers was also at its zenith. Hundreds of new varieties appeared, their names like a roll call of the most beloved people of the time, and specific meanings followed.

The Empress Josephine gathered together an extraordinary collection of roses in her gardens at Malmaison. Being a fashion icon, she simultaneously helped secure their reputation as the most popular and romantic flower of all time. Both she and her garden are remembered in the names of two exquisite roses. Perhaps better forgotten is the unromantic rumour that she carried a rose with her at all times – to hide her rotting teeth when she laughed.

Put on thick gloves to entwine a bedhead with trails of roses for an unforgettably romantic wedding night. Tiny hidden tubes of water ensure that at least the roses will stay fresh till morning. These are multiflora roses, which symbolize grace. On pages 80–1 blood-red roses whisper 'I love you' and open white blooms say 'I am worthy of you' (incidentally, red and white roses together symbolize unity). Secrecy is a full rose above two buds, a striped rose denotes variety, musk roses reflect capricious beauty, a cabbage rose is love's ambassador, and a full-blown rose, like a woman at the peak of her loveliness, says 'you are beautiful'.

Right: Roses (Rosa 'Bobbie James')
Previous pages, from left: Roses (Rosa 'Courage', 'Iceberg', 'Charles de Mills', 'Ferdinand Pichard', 'Felicia', 'Louise Odier' and 'Susan'

Deep red camellias carry the passionate message 'you are a flame in my heart', which was moderated to 'unpretending excellence' in some floral dictionaries.

Camellias

One of the most popular operas *La Traviata* is based on Alexandre Dumas's novel *La Dame aux camélias*. It, in turn, was based on the real-life story of a nineteenth-century Parisian courtesan called Madeleine du Plessis (a name that blossomed into Violetta Valery for Verdi's masterpiece), whose leitmotif was the camellia. Apparently scented flowers made the real Madeleine cough (a precursor, perhaps, to her famous, fatal consumption), and she chose camellias in the first place simply because they have no perfume. In Verdi's opera she wears camellias instead of the jewels she has been forced to sell. In reality, she carried a bouquet of camellias every evening and signalled her 'availability' by holding white flowers for twenty-five days of the month and red flowers for the rest. Different meanings were given to each flower colour. As well as Madeleine du Plessis's personal signals, white camellias signified 'you are adorable' or 'perfected loveliness', and red ones 'you are a flame in my heart' or 'unpretending excellence'. Pink flowers said 'longing for you' or conveyed the calmer sentiment of admiration.

When camellias arrived in the West a hundred years or so earlier, they had already been cherished in their native China for centuries. They went on to become one of the most popular flowers of the era and even received the endorsement of the Empress Josephine who grew them at her famous garden at Malmaison. She was a great style-setter and soon the camellia, cut short and bound to wires, appeared in every well-groomed coiffure or bosom across Europe.

Camellias are now rarely seen as cut flowers, but a flowering camellia plant is one of the most elegant gifts imaginable. The plants are very happy to grow in a pot and this solves their rather fussy soil requirements. Within a few years you should be able to use the plant to supply your own cut flowers. Here freshly cut stems of Camellia have been simply heaped into a shallow bowl of water. A few leaves were removed to focus attention on the flowers.

Camellias (Camellia japonica)

Tulips

Tulips generally represent fame, but red ones are a declaration of love. Striped tulips announce 'you have beautiful eyes' and yellow symbolize hopeless love. Love-lies-bleeding – more optimistically – says hopeless but not heartless. Flowers for an unattainable diva.

The fourteenth-century Persian poet Hafis was waxing lyrical about the tulip long before it was known in the West. His verse used the wild red flowers symbolically, in passionate declarations of love. That message was unchanged when the language of flowers was in its heyday some five hundred years later, but by then the tulip had been through an extraordinary transformation.

Tulips reached Vienna in 1554 and Holland in 1593, brought by travelling merchants and scholars. The rest, as they say, is history. Neither before nor since has a flower had such a huge impact on economics. Speculation based on tulip bulbs became a form of financial brokerage but many more fortunes were lost than made, and the tulip began to appear in the law courts rather than the royal court.

Striped tulips were especially praised as the stripes seemed to appear by magic (we now think that they are caused by a virus). These tulips carried the message 'you have beautiful eyes', perhaps because the stripes resemble eyes next to the fringed 'lashes' of the petals.

'Tulipmania' came to an end in 1637 when the Dutch government outlawed speculation. The tulip had become the plaything of the rich but it had destroyed many people on the way – one dealer even froze to death while his bulbs lay cosseted under his blankets. Yellow tulips were later chosen to represent hopeless love, as experienced by thousands of such tragically obsessed speculators.

Love-lies-bleeding is a member of the mostly red-flowering *Amaranthus* genus, all of which were thought to staunch the flow of blood. The sixteenth-century herbalist Gerard admits that this might be because red flowers look like they ought to 'stop bloud'. In reality, they were completely hopeless at the job, and love would have continued to lie bleeding if they had anything to do with it. They may be hopeless, through no fault of their own, but they are certainly not heartless.

Tulips are as popular today as they have ever been but, thankfully, their price has stabilized. They make great cut flowers and their stems gyrate enticingly around each other over the course of their vase life. I can never see why anyone would want to find a way to stop this process or even wire the poor flowers. They look wonderful in masses of single colours heaped into metal or glass bowls or in vivid multi-colours mixed with carefree abandon.

Tulips can also be arranged in ways reminiscent of the exquisite eighteenth-century tulipières, developed when the flowers were too expensive to use in anything but the tiniest quantities. You can do this by placing single stems in a formally arranged group of slim-necked vases that emphasize the flowers' natural sensuality. However, here I have tied the tulips in a lavish bunch, wrapped in tissue and ribbons – an irresistible token of love.

Tulips (Tulipa) and love-lies-bleeding (Amaranthus caudatus)

Glory lilies & flytraps

Glory lilies symbolize the sublime union of lover and the beloved. Insect-eating flytraps are less sophisticated, with their rejoinder of 'caught at last'!

Glory lilies are exquisite flowers readily available in commercial flower markets but, perhaps because of their fragility, rarely seen in shops. They last very well as a cut flower and even longer as a growing plant. Arrange them in small bunches or individually so their sensual curves are clearly visible.

Flytraps come in many varieties. These two examples catch insects by tempting them into a pool of digestive juices. Here I cut a few lidded capsules from a *Nepenthes* plant and submerged some *Sarracenia* pods in the vase so the water magnified them to even more frightening effect. Aesthetically they may be an acquired taste but what a perfect conversation piece for a hen party or stag night.

Glory lilies (Gloriosa superba 'Rothschildiana') and flytraps (Nepenthes alata and Sarracenia)

We must travel to its original home, the exotic subcontinent of India, to explore the symbolism of the glory lily. The flower is mentioned in many old Tamil *Sangam* poems, which tell of the mountains where the lily grows and where Indian lovers were inclined to meet (the plant's preference for lower altitudes reassuringly intimates that lovers did not have to climb too high before consummating their passion). One beautiful poem tells of a girl who finds a glory lily tuber washed down by heavy rains from the mountains owned by her beloved. She plants it in her garden as a symbol of their union.

In this and similar poems the colours of the lily's petals – vibrant vermilion-pink leaping from a golden yellow base – are passionately compared to the lamps and fires lit by lovers to warm the chill mountain air. The petals' sensuous curves allude to the ornamental rings and bangles recklessly discarded in the heat of the moment. All rather intense for the genteel world of the language of flowers, and so the carnivorous flytrap bounds into view, like the ubiquitous maiden aunt in an EM Forster novel, to dissipate rising passion with the cheery but tactless comment 'caught at last!' It is surprising that a flower with such a sinister appearance and grisly purpose should end up yoked to this jolly-sounding phrase, but the allusion will be appreciated by all bar one – the hapless fly!

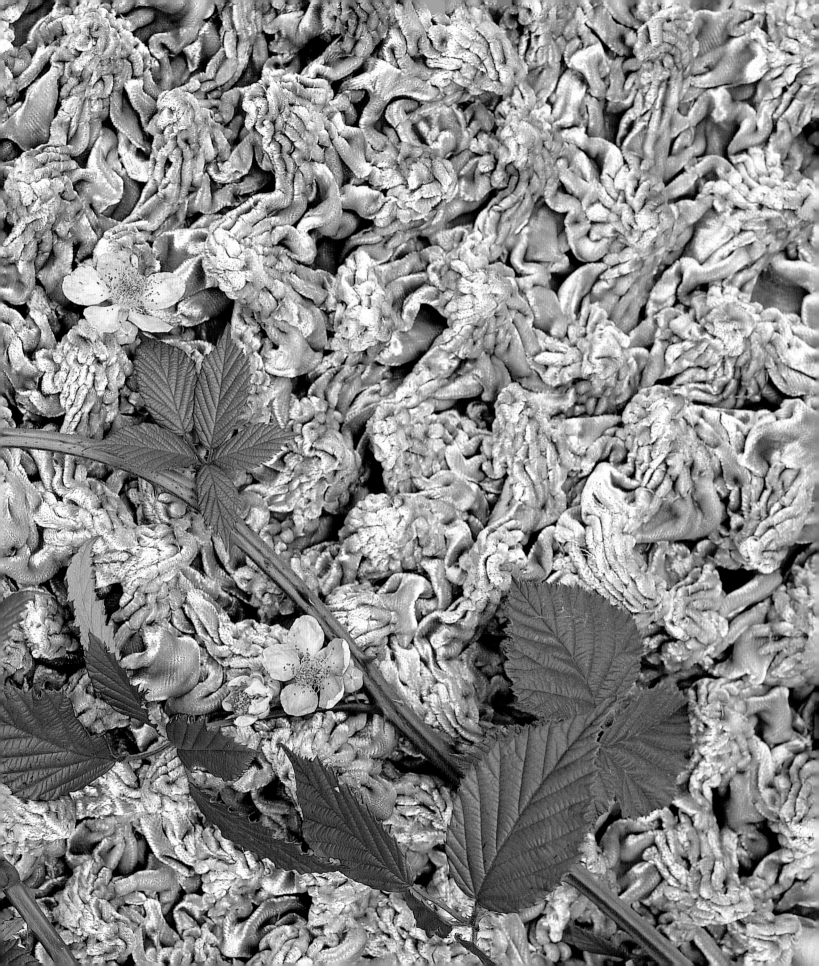

egotism

vanity

conceit

persecution

hauteur

disdain

cruelty

caprice

steadfastness

infamy

lust

Anger, bitterness & passion

Tulips, hellebores & beech

Fame is represented by tulips, a lovers' tryst by beech, while hellebores signify scandal and calumny… a trio to intrigue, captivate and set tongues wagging.

This rich combination of flowers and leaves tells a contemporary tale. The tulips are the starting point, as they are linked with fame and renown – highly appropriate as these aristocratic flowers caused a sensation when they first travelled west from Persia to Vienna in 1554 with the Austrian ambassador to the Persian court. They quickly spread further and, like the Baroque version of a PR dream, their fame went before them. Soon all of Europe was ablaze with 'tulipmania' and fortunes were made and lost speculating on bulbs of desirable forms.

Hellebores add the inevitable touch of scandal and calumny to this tale of success. As a family they are dangerously poisonous plants but, in ancient times, they were used to rid children of worms. One potential side effect was the unfortunate demise of the child as well as the worms. A classical explanation of their symbolism lies in the use of hellebores by the shepherd Melampus. According to Greek tradition, he realized the plant's healing properties by observing its effect on his goats. Later he used it to cure the three daughters of King Proteus of mental derangement by dosing them with the milk of goats that had eaten the plant. These ill-fated young ladies had been condemned to run around naked while deprived of all senses for making fun of a statue. The punishment might seem disproportionate to the crime but it was certainly scandalous.

Finally, the story needs a hint of romance and for this we add beech. Why it should have come to signify a lovers' tryst is not immediately obvious. Perhaps it is linked to the tradition of carving lovers' graffiti upon the trunks of beech trees – a practice popular since Roman times. The Romans had a romantic proverb linked to it: *crescunt illae; crescent amores* (as these letters grow, so shall our love).

Another meaning given to beech is prosperity. This is linked to the beech tree's removal of competitors by casting so deep a shade that everything growing nearby dies – a ruthless way of guaranteeing its own success. This adds a contemporary warning to our tale: the famous beauty has courted scandal, enjoyed a romantic liaison and, in these days of celebrity gossip, someone has profited from the affair.

Hellebores are best cut when the flowers are mature rather than freshly opened. These specimens have already set seed, so are tough and long lasting. Place the freshly cut ends in about 2 cm (1 in) of boiling water and allow the water to cool. Then put the whole flower stem in a deep bucket of cold water so the flowers are completely submerged. Left overnight like this, the flowers will be fully conditioned and ready to arrange. If they do droop, a complete dip in cool water will revive them.

I have arranged them casually in a glass dish with sprays of beech leaves and tulip heads. The key is to make a framework of foliage and then add the flower heads to anchor it all in place.

Tulips (Tulipa 'Queen of the Night'), Lenten hellebores (Helleborus x hybridus) and copper beech (Fagus sylvatica Atropurpurea Group)

Hydrangeas

Unsuspecting hydrangeas have come to be associated
with an astonishing number of thoroughly undesirable
characteristics: they represent vanity, boastfulness,
heartlessness and even frigidity.

Hydrangeas are available practically all year round in virtually every hue imaginable. But I also like bundles of the scruffier autumn flowers in all their changeling shades of flame or subtle pewter. Hydrangeas as cut flowers benefit from having the bottom 2.5 cm (1 in) of their freshly cut stems placed in boiling water for a few minutes before placing in deep cool water. If the flowers wilt, re-cut them and repeat the boiling water treatment. Or, if all else fails, place the whole stem and head in cool water for an hour or two.

Arrange hydrangeas simply as I have here, massed in a large bowl, or use them grouped in mixed arrangements to add substance and strong blocks of colour.

Hydrangea pot plants need lots of water and would even prefer to stand in a few centimetres of water rather than dry out.

Hydrangeas (Hydrangea macrophylla)

When hydrangeas first arrived from America in 1788 they had an impressive welcome at London's docks. For years horticulturalists had been trying to find a way to change the natural colours of flowers and here, apparently, was a plant that could inexplicably change colour at will. It was many years before this 'trick' was linked to the acidity of the soil in which the plant is grown, meanwhile rumours of wizardry – combined with the plant's unusually showy flowers and excessive demands for water during the voyage – had already established an enduring link with vanity and boastfulness.

If these affiliations were unfair, then its adoption as a symbol of heartlessness and frigidity was iniquitous. Through no fault of its own, each hydrangea flower head has only a few fertile florets mixed with many sterile ones. This perplexed learned botanists as much as its colour flexibility, and they were unable to decide among themselves which bit was flower, sepal, anther or stigma. Sexual irregularity did nothing to improve the poor plant's reputation.

You might say that this lovely flower has been misconstrued, and one dictionary of flower meanings seems to set out to make amends by according hydrangeas the grateful denotation 'thank you for understanding'. You can see why!

Foxgloves & rugosa roses

Deliver a scathing attack with these flowers. Foxgloves represent insincerity and self-ambition while rugosa roses suggest 'beauty is your only attraction'.

These two beautiful blooms have unfortunately ugly meanings. In the mists of time they may have done something to deserve their ascribed associations, but today they are fully redeemed.

Foxgloves are handsome flowers, but they are also notoriously noxious. No animal except the bee touches them and he is probably very careful. They were hugely popular in ancient folk medicine but it was well known that foxgloves would proverbially kill or cure. A tea made from the leaves was a popular treatment for dropsy, an especially agonizing form of fluid retention where the patient probably hardly cared whether he lived or died anyway.

In 1785 a physician, William Withering, wrote a revolutionary book called *An Account of the Foxglove*, which recorded its healing credentials. He realized that foxgloves contained a substance that had a primary effect on the heart. This drug, digitalis, is still in use today. He also recommended smaller doses in medicines, which helped reduce the number of fatalities – although people were still killing themselves with foxglove tea well into the nineteenth century. This might imply a link with unreliability – but insincerity and self-ambition? For that we need to look at its common name. *Foxes glofa* were mentioned in 1000AD in a Norse legend that claimed foxes wore the flowers on their paws as gloves, to make an even stealthier entrance into the hen roost.

Rugosa roses are native to China, Korea and Japan. They were introduced to Britain as Japanese roses in 1796 by a company called Key and Kennedy of Hammersmith. They are beautiful and vigorous, but the symbolic language of flowers decided, presumably because of their deadly battery of thorns, that their looks were their only attraction. Rose lovers may not agree.

Rugosa roses are a bit of a menace to use in flower arranging but the effort of putting on strong gloves is repaid in full. Cut long branches, as I have here, or snip off clusters of flowers to use in low arrangements. Thorny-stemmed flowers *must* go into an arrangement first: you will shred everything else if you push them in later on. It also allows you to get them to sit satisfactorily without damaging more delicate specimens. I arranged the roses here in a tall glass goblet vase and added a handful of foxgloves afterwards. Grouping the foxgloves is a great way to make a few stems look more generous.

Foxgloves (Digitalis purpurea) *and rugosa roses* (Rosa 'Roseraie de l'Haÿ')

This combination of flowers tells a bitter tale of frustrated love.

Slipper orchids represent an unreliable capricious beauty, and wallflowers symbolize a long-suffering lover's fidelity in the face of adversity.

Unusual flower combinations are always interesting. While these unexpected bedfellows have a common colour tone, the soft velvety texture of the wallflowers contrasts with and complements the orchid's waxy formality.

I used only two orchid stems – a subtle allusion to a pair of slippers – and a handful of wallflowers. The wallflowers went in first, in a loose way, and then I added the more delicate orchids, close together for maximum impact.

Datura flowers (deceitful charms), foxgloves (insincerity, see page 98) and camomile (patience) convey similar messages.

Wallflowers (Erysimum cheiri) *and slipper orchids* (Cypripedium venustum)

Wallflowers & slipper orchids

The marriage of urbane orchids and rustic wallflowers is as incongruous as the unhappy union they symbolize. Wallflowers are simple innocent flowers seen in country gardens or clinging to cliff faces and old walls, hence their common name. Orchids, on the other hand, are cosmopolitan degenerates associated with lust and lucre.

Slipper orchids are properly called *Cypripedium*, a reference to Cyprus where Venus was born and worshipped and, apparently, where harlots were plentiful. In France the flowers were known as *sabots de Venus* and, like all orchids, thought to be an aphrodisiac. Orchids also hybridize enthusiastically – a trait readily likened to promiscuous behaviour. And so, whimsical and wanton, slipper orchids came to represent life's capricious beauties.

Wallflowers derive their meaning from an ancient tale of devoted love. A maiden was locked in a tall tower by her father to prevent her from seeing her lover. Her devoted suitor visited daily, hoping to glimpse his beloved at her window. She finally saw him far below and tried to climb down to him by clutching the wallflowers covering the tower walls but, unfortunately, she fell to her death. Wallflowers then came to represent love that stays faithful through all adversity.

Clematis & snake's head fritillaries

Representing vacuous beauty or a more sinister artifice, clematis remind us that appearances can be deceptive. Snake's head fritillaries symbolize the feelings of persecution and vexation caused by such shallow charmers.

In its wild form clematis (*Clematis vitalba*) is used in both homeopathy and Bach flower remedies to deal with daydreamers – empty-headed, impractical sorts who can never remember anything and need to concentrate more. To them the clematis is a kindred spirit, growing, given half a chance, to the tops of trees and then hanging around in a tangled, confused mass of misty flowers. However, it has also come to be associated with artifice; perhaps its climbing habit is more manipulative and conniving than it seems. The appearance of mindlessness may be a pretence and the beauty not quite so dumb after all.

Whatever their true mental capabilities, life with such an apparently asinine companion could be vexing. This is depicted by snake's head fritillaries, which are associated with persecution. We can only speculate on the origins of this affiliation. Is it because of the visual similarity of the petals to a venomous snake? Is it a reflection of the origin of the flower's name? Fritillary's species name, *meleagris*, is Greek for guinea fowl, which has a similar chequered pattern to its feathers and might well feel persecuted by those who find them a great culinary delicacy. Today the flowers themselves are the ones persecuted as their natural habitats are destroyed by intensive farming methods.

Fritillaries are a great favourite of mine and snake's head fritillaries in particular. They are ideal garden plants and can often be bought, in season, as small plants in full flower. Enjoy them like this indoors and then plant them out in the garden as the flowers fade. Snake's head fritillaries like damp spots and are quite capable of moving themselves around a garden until they find a place that appeals. Once established, there's no harm in picking a few stems, as I have here. Place them in water in an interesting container like this old finial base, which holds them vertically and allows them to look as they do when growing naturally.

Clematis are another popular garden plant with infinite varieties. The *montana* species is one of the most rampant and certainly will not miss a few trails if you cut them off carefully. Clematis can also be bought as flowering plants to be appreciated indoors before planting out.

Snake's head fritillaries (Fritillaria meleagris) *and a trail of clematis* (Clematis montana 'Elizabeth')

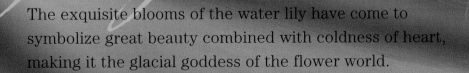

Nymphaea

The exquisite blooms of the water lily have come to symbolize great beauty combined with coldness of heart, making it the glacial goddess of the flower world.

Water lilies

The perfect beauty of water lilies has been revered since ancient times. They take their botanical name from the Greek water deities, the nymphs, who were said to be eternally young, beautiful and virginal. This interminable chastity was no doubt the link with rumours of coldheartedness – the Ancient Greeks even believed that water lilies had anti-aphrodisiac qualities. Somehow this reputation stuck and, by the Middle Ages, a paste of ground water lily root was recommended to preserve the celibacy of priests and nuns. We can only speculate as to the method of application.

By the pre-Raphelite era, the language of flowers had become an integral part of artistic symbolism. In his painting Hylas and the Nymphs (1896) Waterhouse chose water lilies to underline the coldheartedness of the nymphs. They are pictured luring the handsome youth Hylas into the chilly depths of their lily-covered lake. The fate of Hylas could have been either an abrupt death by drowning or everlasting sexual bliss – though the nymphs' chaste reputation combined with the water lilies' symbolism would imply the worst.

The water lily, like several other flowers, has a male and female stage in its reproductive cycle. In the male stage, the flower opens daily with generous quantities of pollen on its anthers to attract insects from far and near. After a few days the female stage begins and the flower opens with shimmering, pollenless anthers surrounding a sinister pool of liquid. Visiting insects slip and slide down the smooth anthers into the pool and drown. As they do so, pollen washes off them, settles on the submerged female stigma and fertilizes the flower. If ever there were a callous beauty in the flower world, the water lily is surely it.

Water lilies and lotus are now regularly available as cut flowers. Their habit of closing and opening in response to light and temperature makes them an unreliable choice for a specific event but a thrilling houseguest when you can enjoy such antics over a period of time. Arrange them en masse floating in water in a pseudo-natural way, as I have here. Adding large leaves would increase the illusion. Alternatively, place them in small-necked vases grouped together or singly and enjoy the contortions of the stems as well as the movement of the flowers.

Water lilies (Nymphaea)

Forget-me-nots & anemones

Forget-me-nots symbolize true love and the human longing for lasting love, while anemones are associated with abandonment, the pain of parting and the transience of that same love.

How did two pretty flowers come to depict such sorrow? Of the pair, the forget-me-not is rather more optimistic. Its name has been around, in several languages, since at least the fifteenth century. The most excruciating tale of its origin concerns a riverside tragedy. A knight fell into the water while picking the flowers for his lady and, before being swept away, shouted: 'Forget me not.' A slightly more bearable version tells how this little flower forgot her own name on the day of creation. That evening, seeing the Lord walking in the garden, she shyly asked him what she was called: 'Forget-me-not' was his reply.

The anemone's curriculum vitae is unlikely to lift the gloom. Its name is derived from the Greek for windy habitation (where some species thrive). One story of its creation tells how Zephyrus, the god of the west wind, fell in love with a nymph who was turned into an anemone by his jealous wife to remove temptation. These are the flower's first links with the emotions of separation and ephemeral love – upon which it has based its career – and with its common name of zephyr flower.

Other myths tell how anemones sprang either from Aphrodite's tears at the death of her beloved Adonis, or from Adonis's blood, which he shed as he died – again the heartbreaking association with parting and transience. Aphrodite apparently made a surprisingly swift recovery, reinforcing the anemone's melancholy links with love's impermanence.

Forget-me-not and anemone's sombre combined message is timeless: our need to love deeply makes parting unbearable.

Forget-me-nots are not often sold in flower shops, which is a pity. When you do buy or pick some, remove as many of their leaves as you can (without spoiling their appearance) to prevent water loss. This also helps aesthetically, as the flowers are inclined to hide behind the leaves. Arrange forget-me-nots on their own, as I have here, the stems swirled loosely into a bowl of water, for a moody look. For a more traditional arrangement, place them in small vases. Forget-me-nots make beautiful companions for other tiny spring flowers: adding lilies-of-the-valley would be an appropriate combination as they represent the return of happiness. The composite message would be both optimistic and poignant.

In spite of their tragic associations, anemones are deservedly popular garden and cut flowers. They, too, make eye-catching arrangements on their own. Here, stems are held separately in glass phials to emphasize their loneliness, but their heads look equally wonderful en masse in contemporary arrangements. I prefer to use self-coloured anemones but they are often sold in bunches of bright mixed colours, which have a frivolity that belies their doleful symbolism. In contrast to their bold garden cousins, little wild wood anemones (*Anemone blanda* or *A. nemorosa*) represent anticipation and expectation.

Left: Anemones (Anemone coronaria)
Opposite: Forget-me-nots (Myosotis dissitiflora)

109

These simple flowers have a well-known meaning:
blatant egotism, vanity and self-love.

Narcissi and most soft-stemmed spring flowers prefer to be placed in vases of water rather than arranged in floral foam. The soft stems tend to make the latter impossible anyway. I love to see narcissi arranged without pretence, and this collection of white containers allows them to look much as they do when growing. A few strands of long grass would give an even more naturalistic appearance. Try them massed in tall glass cylinders where their characteristic stems become part of the arrangement, too.

Alternative flowers with a similar message are hydrangeas (boastfulness and heartlessness, see page 97) and pomegranate blossom (conceit and pride).

*Pheasant's eye narcissi (*Narcissus poeticus *var.* recurvus)

Narcissi

The tale of the beautiful Greek youth Narcissus is a familiar one. Ovid describes his great beauty and how he broke Echo's heart by his constant rejection of her love. Poor Echo faded away until only her voice remained. As a punishment, the gods led Narcissus to a pool where he saw his reflection for the first time and became transfixed by his own beauty. In his grief at falling in love with his reflection, Narcissus wasted away, his gaze fixed on the water. Where his once beautiful body lay, narcissus flowers grew.

The name narcissus might originate from the Greek word for narcotic, as the scent of narcissi was thought to have the power to overwhelm and reduce mortals to a state of complete stupor. In much the same way, egotism and self-absorption can overtake a person's life. Narcissus flowers can be a gentle reminder of that particular danger as the flowers incline their heads downwards as if still desperately trying to catch a glimpse of their own reflection.

Tuberose, nettles & brambles

This trio sends a message of biting censure. Nettles make an allegation of cruelty, brambles hint at suffering and tuberose suggest dangerous pleasures.

Where do you begin with such a caustic collection? The most readily available is tuberose, which could be used to chastise or intimidate. In its native Mexico tuberose essential oil was used by the Aztecs to flavour the chocolate to which they were addicted. This makes a satisfying link with the flower's meaning of dangerous pleasures, be they addictive love or fattening chocolate.

When the tuberose was brought back to Spain, the essential oil was used extensively in perfume and was also thought to be an aphrodisiac. By this time tuberose had also been discovered growing naturally in Hawaii, where the flowers were used to make the traditional leis worn by topless natives. Both associations undoubtedly added to the tuberose's notorious reputation.

The meanings accorded to nettles and brambles are self-evident. Rarely was a plant more cruel than the stinging nettle, and brambles certainly pose difficulties if you want to get past them. Their sharp thorns have long been associated with the suffering of Christ, and the berries with the fruits of his passion and death.

The scent of tuberose makes them a wonderful, sensual gift. Some floral dictionaries give them the alternative meaning of voluptuousness, which is less condemning. I like to arrange tuberose gracefully in tall vases that support the stems in a loose vertical bunch. They will last much longer if you remove dead flowers daily, allowing the buds to open all along the stem.

To convey the strongest message possible you will need nettles and brambles, too. Wear thick gloves to cut them and then treat them as you would any cultivated flower. The fruits of brambles are especially decorative but pick the stems before the fruits are ripe or they will drop off and leave a stain where they fall.

Tuberose (Polianthes tuberosa), nettles (Urtica dioica) and brambles (Rubus fructicosus)

healing

reassurance

constancy

repentance

felicity

bliss

serenity

partnership

commitment

enlightenment

restoration

Forgiveness, happiness & contentment

If you are lucky enough to have an old apple tree growing in your garden, try cutting a few branches of beautiful blossom in spring. I love their gnarled knobbly shapes and like to emphasize these when I arrange them indoors. One or more tall slim vases will do this perfectly and let you create a graceful airy arrangement that might have come straight from an oriental screen. You can achieve similar effects with other types of blossom but be aware of their different meanings: cherry blossom implies spiritual beauty, almond blossom symbolizes hope but crab-apple blossom denotes ill-temper, so be warned.

Apple blossom (Malus domestica) *and lichen*

Apple blossom & lichen

Dejection and solitude, represented by lichen, can sometimes lead to repentance, symbolized by apple blossom – paving the way to forgiveness.

Apple trees grew in two famous mythical gardens. In the Garden of Eden, Adam and Eve came to awareness after eating the forbidden fruit of The Tree of the Knowledge of Good and Evil. They repented but still lost their idyllic lifestyle. Sin had been born. This left the apple tree with a heavy legacy of responsibility that is reflected in its floral symbolism: apples represent temptation and apple blossom, repentance.

In Hera's sacred garden near Mount Olympus, there was a golden apple tree guarded by a dragon. This was a wedding present from Mother Earth when Hera married her own twin brother Zeus. One of its golden apples, mysteriously inscribed 'To the most beautiful', caused a dreadful row between three competing goddesses until a hapless mortal, Paris, was given the unenviable task of choosing who really deserved it. From this episode came two meanings, that of preference in floral dictionaries, plus the phrase 'an apple of discord' to describe an irritant.

Apple branches sometimes host a grey moss-like growth called lichen. This attractive oddity is actually two organisms, an alga and a fungus, living in perfect symbiotic harmony. They prefer to grow in isolated areas where the air is pure, and are often seen at high altitudes – even above the snow line. They suggest solitude and, by default, dejection.

Together these flowers represent a happy and secure relationship: hyacinths symbolize constant and unchanging love, lily of the valley implies a return of happiness and Solomon's seal confirms the permanence of the whole affair.

Lily of the valley, Solomon's seal & hyacinths

In Greek mythology handsome Hyacinthus was the paramour of the god Apollo. Zeyphyrus, god of the west wind, also appreciated Hyacinthus's various attractions, but his love was unrequited. Revenge was inevitable and, as Apollo and Hyacinthus were at play, a malicious gust of wind fatally redirected the discus thrown by Apollo towards the head of Hyacinthus. Where drops of his dead lover's blood fell, the distraught Apollo caused sweet-scented hyacinths to grow. With their upturned petals the very image of his curling locks, the flowers symbolize Hyacinthus's beauty and Apollo's eternal love.

Since ancient times Solomon's seal has been hailed as a healer of cuts, broken bones and bruises. Its related floral symbolism of healing in relationships was perhaps inevitable.

The main healing ingredient in Solomon's seal is convallarin, also found in lily of the valley. The herbalist Gerard sang the praises of this plant in the sixteenth century, claiming that it could 'comfort the heart'. It has, however, to be treated with respect as it is highly poisonous. Both beneficial and deleterious, there is a link with the importance of making the right choice. Lily of the valley signifies a good decision and the ensuing return of happiness, particularly in matters of the heart.

Lily of the valley and Solomon's seal make very happy companions, visually and symbolically, for the more readily available hyacinths, and the combined scents are totally delicious. When arranging a monochromatic collection of flowers like this, it can be interesting to keep foliage to a bare minimum. The hyacinths are perfectly happy to be denuded and, indeed, last longer without their strappy leaves. I also like to arrange these flowers as simply as possible in separate containers. In common with most soft-stemmed spring flowers they prefer to be placed in water rather than florist's foam. I find that lily of the valley lasts better when cut and placed in warm water before becoming part of the final arrangement.

Lily of the valley (Convallaria majalis), *hyacinths* (Hyacinthus orientalis) *and Solomon's seal* (Polygonatum multiflorum)

An old Arab legend relates how Adam and Eve, the very first couple, brought only three plants with them when they were expelled from the Garden of Eden: figs, dates and myrtle. Both the Ancient Greeks and Romans associated myrtle with love and marriage, and it was dedicated to their goddesses of love, Aphrodite and Venus. Both goddesses were guardians of marriage and many Roman brides wore garlands of myrtle in their hair.

Myrtle wreaths were also to be seen on the heads of the rather less nubile male municipal council members in Ancient Greece, where they represented willingness to compromise and reach a mutual agreement – in or out of marriage.

Not surprisingly, myrtle became a traditional element in bridal bouquets. Perhaps its most famous exponent was Queen Victoria who decreed that the sprig of myrtle from her own

Myrtle & phlox

Myrtle has been the symbol of love and contented married life since ancient times, and phlox, with its meaning of the perfect unity of hearts and souls, completes the wish for wedded bliss.

wedding bouquet should be rooted and grown to supply future royal brides in perpetuity. It was and it has. But the Christian Church was at first reluctant to allow this blatantly pagan symbol through its doors. Its case was helped when it was pointed out that the aromatic leaves were, like Christ on the cross, perforated… albeit minutely.

The story of phlox involved an intrepid Belfast man, Thomas Drummond. He was the curator of the city's botanical gardens and set out on a solo plant-collecting trek through north-west America in 1831. He was single-minded in his quest and overcame the most appalling hardships. He survived, among other things, a shipboard epidemic of cholera, encounters with the indigenous – and indignant – animal population, agonizing boils, a paralysed hand and a severe winter on his own, which he survived only by gradually ingesting his deerskin coat. He died suddenly in Cuba in 1835, and the last plant he sent home was the annual phlox, named *Phlox drummondii* in his memory. The language of flowers honoured this intrepid plantsman by forever associating phlox with his single-mindedness.

Aromatic myrtle and scented phlox combine to make symbolically auspicious candlesticks for a wedding. Start by cutting small sprigs of myrtle and, using binding wire (which you can buy from any floral supplier), bind them to a piece of bamboo. Leave the top 2–3 cm (1 inch) bare, so that you can push it into the base of a candle. The candlestick base is a heavy saucer of floral foam held in place with a layer of chicken wire and floral tape. Insert the myrtle-covered bamboo into the foam and add a few taller pieces of myrtle, pushed in beside it and bound to it, to keep the whole thing vertical. Disguise the floral foam by inserting massed flower heads of white phlox.
*Myrtle (*Myrtus communis*) and white phlox (*Phlox paniculata*)*

Cattleya orchid

This cattleya orchid corsage is intended to flatter with its meaning of mature charms – charms that have reached the peak of perfection rather than having simply grown old.

Cattleya orchids were relative rarities at the beginning of the nineteenth century. They were first grown in the UK by tropical plant enthusiast William Cattley in 1818 but, alas, his first imports all flowered and died within a year. Several years later he rediscovered some healthier specimens in Brazil, after a serendipitous sighting of a cattleya corsage on the décolletage of a South American heiress at a Parisian ball. Cattleyas quickly became fashionable and were adopted by the language of flowers to represent mature charms.

Cattleyas certainly have a sensual voluptuousness more suited to the sophisticate than the debutante, but their link with maturity must also stem from the long association between orchids and sexuality. The name orchid originates from the Ancient Greek word for testicles (a reference to the shape of the roots of some species). This brazen comparison, coupled with the historical use of ground orchid root as an aphrodisiac, would have been thought too indelicate for all but the well informed. The 'mature' epithet might simply have been an elegant euphemism for 'adults only'!

Although these links all appear to be connected with advancing years, it is important to remember that maturity involves a tantalizing ripening or blossoming process, otherwise the compliment might be received with less enthusiasm than it is given.

There are not many occasions when a woman would wear a corsage today, but it is still a very glamorous gift. Making a corsage is generally a job for a professional florist, but if you use only one or two large blooms, as I have here, it is a feasible project for any enthusiastic amateur. First you need to push a wire up the stem of each flower and secure and cover it with green floral tape. (You can buy floral wires and tape from most flower shops or wholesalers.) The wire strengthens the stem and makes it more pliable, while the tape seals it and prevents moisture loss. Make the corsage by twisting the wires together into a shape that flatters each flower best. Wrap the corsage in damp tissue and keep it in a cool place until needed.

Orchid corsage (Cattleya)

Pink roses symbolize perfect happiness. Choose them on days when you want to sing 'all's well in my world!'

Roses of any colour are popular gifts of love but the long-stemmed varieties are often difficult to deal with in arrangements. They look so unlike anything that grows in a real garden. I prefer to let the flowers open and then cut off the heads to float in a large bowl of water. This makes a few expensive stems look infinitely more impressive. Beautiful sprays of garden roses like those pictured are much easier to arrange. The key to success here is the choice of container. This striking contemporary bowl of grey-blue glass, which looks almost molten, makes a wonderful contrast to the pink petals.

Pink roses (Rosa 'Cornelia')

Pink roses

The ancient Persian word for flower – *gul* – also means rose and it is almost the same as the word for spirit. This is hardly surprising as roses have been linked with every human emotion, and used to delight every human sense since time began.

Roses have also been associated with physical as well as spiritual wellbeing. In Arabia they were recorded as a treatment for tuberculosis. In the sixteenth century the herbalist Gerard advised that distilled water of roses could be used to strengthen the heart and refresh the spirits, while fresh roses could induce sleep 'through their sweet and pleasant smell'. Rose-hip syrup was given to babies as a source of vitamin C well into the twentieth century, and rose-water still refreshes many beautiful complexions.

Roses are eternally bonded to a life of health, happiness and contentment. In the lexicons of floral symbolism, pink roses were specifically singled out to represent the enviable bliss of such a life. It was a perfect choice. If red roses reflect the heated fluster of exciting but unsettling passions, then pink roses echo the gentler glow on a healthy cheek and a serene mind that has found security and peace in its life and its love.

Sweet-scented stocks have a surfeit of pleasing associations:
they represent lasting beauty and symbolize a happy life.

As cut flowers, stocks are short-lived, so their link with anything lasting is somewhat ironic. They are a member of the Brassicaceae family, which also includes cabbages and, if the water in which they are arranged is not changed frequently, their relationship becomes all too evident. The trick is to arrange them quickly and simply. Here I have placed the stems in a vase and allowed them to fall entirely naturally.

Send a similar message with perennial sweet peas (lasting pleasures) or a bunch of full-blown roses ('you are beautiful', see page 82).

Stocks (Matthiola 'Cassis')

Stocks

Many varieties of stocks have been developed by keen gardeners over the years, evidence of centuries of hybridization and proof – if proof were needed – of their enduring popularity.

Stocks appear jointly with violets in some floral history books as the food of choice for poor Io, the unlucky girl who was turned into a white heifer by Zeus. That, as the saying goes, is another story (see page 43), but as a result the Ancient Romans called both flowers violas.

By the sixteenth century the term 'stocks' came into use. Stock gillyflowers were so-called in reference to their thick stock, or stem, and to distinguish them from thinner-stemmed dianthus flowers, which were then known as clove gillyflowers. The common denominator between the two species was their clove-like scent.

In poetry of the Middle Ages stocks were always linked with lasting beauty and a contented life, and were immensely popular in the ornamental gardens that were becoming a feature of desirable homes. Ladies were so keen to be associated with this symbolism that garden stocks were incredibly well tended and cherished as an outward sign that all was well within.

By the nineteenth century they were used to convey the message 'you will always be beautiful to me', making them the perfect gift for devoted couples.

Oats, rushes & achillea

Oats symbolizing music, rushes for calm and docility, and the flowers of achillea to represent a cure for broken hearts – a combination to sustain Shakespeare's claim that music can banish 'care and grief of heart'.

There is an ancient English superstition that oat sheaves should be left out for three weeks before being stacked so that the church bells might ring over them on three consecutive Sundays to cleanse them of any evil. (Up to the Middle Ages, oats had been thought to attract vampires.) The older floral dictionaries give their meaning as the bewitching soul of music, which seems to support this traditional musical connection. Alternatively, the meaning might stem from the less hallowed music of the public house. It was an old European harvest tradition to elect an oats-bride, who would be led into town carrying the last sheaf of oats harvested. There, in the tavern, there would be music and general wassailing until dawn.

Rushes were also an essential part of simple rural life. Their strong and useful pith can be removed and dried to make rush lights by soaking it in left-over cooking fats and greases and wax, if available. These were the sole source of light in most country cottages up until the middle of the nineteenth century and they burnt with a clear smokeless flame. This bright light earned rushes their links with enlightenment, calm and docility.

The benefits of achillea would also have been well known to country folk. One of its common names was 'staunch weed' as its leaves could be crushed and used to stop bleeding. Its name comes from the Greek hero Achilles, who used it to heal his injured soldiers as it is particularly effective for wounds caused by metal. It was often the only available treatment during the American Civil War, with the result that the plant became associated with battle. Because of its then almost miraculous ability to save lives, it also came to be seen as a way to avoid the heartache of bereaved loved ones left at home. A happy example, perhaps, of preventing heartbreak, rather than curing it.

Rushes and edible oats are not strictly plants for the garden or flower shop, but sometimes wild oats are sold in shops and so I have taken the liberty of using them here. They are a beautiful but pernicious weed of arable land, which most landowners would be delighted to see removed, but it is important to ask permission before you pick. The same applies to rushes, which grow wild near water in damp shady spots. Achillea, on the other hand, is available both as a cut flower and as a garden plant in a multitude of colours and types. When arranging these wild flowers it is important not to try too hard or they will appear contrived and uncomfortable. Let them fall in a vase so they look natural and at ease.

Music can also be represented by a bundle of reeds, while olive foliage symbolizes peace.

Oats (Avena fatua), rushes (Juncus effusus) and achillea (Achillea millefolium)

This arrangement is a relaxed interpretation of the classical 'mixed group'. Stems of amaryllis and crown imperials are difficult to insert into floral foam; it is easier to use a vase of deep water for this design. The tall earthenware container is also heavy enough to balance these weighty flowers. I first made a supporting framework from the birch twigs and then added a bed of *Magnolia grandiflora* foliage. The tawny felted undersides of the leaves are really worth seeing so twist them until they show to best effect. Only when you are totally happy with this foliage base should you add the fleshy and easily bruised blooms of amaryllis and crown imperials. I kept them grouped by type in this arrangement to help give it a contemporary feeling.

Crown imperials (Fritillaria imperialis), *amaryllis* (Hippeastrum), Magnolia grandiflora *and birch twigs* (Betula pendula)

Crown imperials, amaryllis, magnolia grandiflora & birch

Crown imperials were first named by the Duke of Tuscany, so they were always destined to have a natural affinity with the *haute monde*. Their native home was in the Western Himalayas and, when they first arrived in Vienna in 1576, they were an immediate hit and quickly became the *sine qua non* of the ornamental gardens that were so popular then with the European nobility.

There is a legend that tells how the flowers used to point upwards until the Lord, seeing how grand and arrogant the plant had become, twisted them back down towards earth. They remained that way, and the copious drops of nectar they produce were said to be tears of humiliation. Some might think that the Lord had already chastized the plant enough with its peculiar and particularly unaristocratic scent.

The amaryllis is another grand flower with an embarrassing personal problem – this time with names, rather than odours. It should properly be called *Hippeastrum* and, to double its degradation, Amaryllis was originally the name of a mere shepherdess. The flowers were discovered in the Andes in the mid-eighteenth century and were brought triumphantly to Europe. They have now completely abandoned their old home and settled into a cosseted lifestyle in the glasshouses of Holland, where they are grown in millions to supply the cut-flower trade.

Magnolia grandiflora is so regal that it is invariably called by its botanical name. It is entitled to behave imperiously: it has been around, quite literally, since the heyday of the *Tyrannosaurus rex*, and was one of the first plants to use insects in its reproductive technique.

By comparison, the birch is a humble pedestrian in this august gathering, even though it was a tree beloved of Celtic and medieval poets, who praised its silvery grace and humility. It will grow absolutely anywhere – a trait that does not endear it to foresters but it does remind us to be more self-effacing.

The crown imperial symbolizes power and pride, amaryllis echoes pride and adds splendid beauty, magnolia is proud and peerless, while simple birch adds vital meekness and grace – flowers for life's success stories.

nostalgia

consolation

solace

recollection

virtue

respect

remorse

regret

loss

faith

departure

Rembrance,
regrets & farewells

Passionflowers, guelder roses & parsley

Passionflowers symbolize faith and spirituality, guelder roses suggest heavenly thoughts, winter and age, while parsley adds lasting pleasures – flowers for those ethereal moments in life.

Passionflowers were discovered by the early Spanish conquistadors in South America. The extraordinary physical make-up of the flower appeared to them like a natural depiction of Christ's passion on the cross: with five anthers to recall his five wounds, plus nail-like stigmata and whip-like tendrils, they were seen as a divine icon. To their eternal shame, the Spanish interpreted the passionflower as a token of sacred authorization for their reign of terror over the peaceful Inca civilization.

Some time around 1568 passionflowers were brought back to Pope Pius V, who declared them miraculous. And from then on the flowers began to be seen increasingly in churches around Europe, carved into woodwork and embroidered on textiles. They symbolized the passionate faith and spiritual beliefs of a whole age.

The story of the guelder rose is similarly set in an age of faith and miracles. A legend tells how the ghost of a young girl wandered the fields she loved until an angel appeared to her and offered her the chance to become a flower and so stay on earth. She asked to become a guelder rose, which, at that time, flowered in the winter. The angel asked her: 'Why do you want to flower when all is dead?', but he granted her request and managed also to persuade the guelder rose to flower in May. Now it blooms at Whitsuntide, a time that celebrates the descent of the Holy Spirit and Christ's Ascension into heaven – a plethora of heavenly thoughts. Its common name, Snowball Tree, adds a more earthly link and underlines its winter symbolism.

The Greeks used parsley to decorate tombs as it was sacred to Persephone, goddess of the underworld. But they also fed it to athletes and horses to give them lasting energy before major trials. It has been an important medicinal herb since Roman times and has helped prolong and improve life's pleasures all along – not least with its lasting effect on bad breath.

The guelder rose has wonderfully decorative lime-green balls of flowers and is widely available in a cultivated form, on extraordinarily long straight branches. Garden forms are much stubbier though equally beautiful. I have placed a bunch of cultivated guelder roses to one side of this slim-necked jug of water and added a meandering trail of passionflowers opposite to balance it. These trails can be cut from a growing plant with no adverse effects. I found this particular stem lasted for almost a month in water, and several new buds opened long after the original flowers had faded.

Finally, the requisite bunch of parsley was pushed into the centre of the arrangement – herbs need not be only for cooking!

Passionflowers (Passiflora caerulea), *guelder* (Viburnum opulus 'Roseum') *and parsley* (Petroselinum crispum)

Lilac (*Syringa vulgaris*) has several similar meanings and, if you add the variations accorded to purple versus white lilac, the list grows longer. The common thread with white lilac seems to be 'youth' and 'memories of youth' or even, in some older flower dictionaries, the 'innocent candour of youth'. As the lilac flowers early in the year, the metaphor of youthfulness is a natural one, but the slightly wistful and nostalgic aspect in its meaning has a few other possible sources: the first is the little-known fact that burning lilac wood results in a smoke with the sweet fragrance of the open flowers – a memory of glorious youth in the blackening dead wood.

A slightly less lugubrious link between lilac and memory might originate from the tradition among early American pioneers of planting bushes in front of their homesteads as a sign of civilization in the wilderness where they struggled to make a life. Lilacs are persistent and will regrow from the old roots of cut-down bushes. They can still be seen where the original farmhouses have long vanished – reminders of a time of youthful optimism and energy.

Take your pick. Either way, white lilac has strong associations with memories of innocent youthful times, and is a great choice when thoughts are to be directed to the happy days of yore.

White lilac

White lilac symbolizes memories of youth and the happy innocence of days long since past.

From a practical point of view it is important to know how to treat lilac. It is available nearly all year around on eerily long bare stems from greenhouse sources. These last best when the bottom 3 cm (1½ in) of the woody stems are lightly bashed with a hammer, then placed in deep fresh water. If they begin to droop prematurely, place the re-cut stems in a bucket holding a few centimetres of boiling water. Allow the water to cool before arranging the lilac in deep water in a vase, either on their own or with other tall flowers.

For an all too brief period in spring, lilac is also available in delicious branchy bundles from garden sources. For these to last any length of time, you need to remove all the leaves and then bash and boil the stems as necessary. If you do not remove the leaves, garden lilac seems to be incapable of supporting both leaves and flowers in a cut state and simply gives up. It looks best arranged, as I have here, on short stems in the generous quantities in which it grows and simply heaped into a large bowl of water.

White lilac (Syringa vulgaris)

In its heyday, the language of flowers would often have been expressed through flowers arranged in this formal style. Today we refer to them as Victorian posies. They are not difficult to make but it is important to prepare all the 'ingredients' before you start. Lay the stems on a table in separate piles for each species. Start with a central flower and simply add flowers in rows of each type until you have built up a domed circle. Take care not to underestimate the quantity of flowers you will need, especially if you are using small-headed flowers, as I have here.

Michaelmas daisies (Aster novi-belgii *varieties*), *raspberries* (Rubus idaeus), *purple verbena* (Verbena bonariensis *and* Verbena x hybrida *'Derby Series') and bay* (Laurus nobilis)

Michaelmas daisies, raspberries, purple verbena & bay

This exquisite little posy conveys feelings of heartfelt sympathy. It also contains four interesting floral characters, beginning with Michaelmas daisies, which flower at the summer's end – a signal of the change of season, rather like the farewell or afterthought they signify.

In Greek mythology, a nymph called Ida pricked her finger while picking raspberries for the infant god Jupiter. Ida is still remembered in their botanical name today but, unfortunately, we cannot tell whether the remorse was supposed to be Ida's, the raspberry bush's or our own.

Verbenas are an ancient flower, their name coming from a generic Roman term for plants used in sacrifice and worship. They are particularly linked with tears, which probably originates from the legend that verbenas grew on Mount Golgotha, where Christ was crucified. Their link with sacrific is an obvious explanation for the story that they grew beneath His cross.

Bay takes us back to Ancient Greece, where Apollo was in hot pursuit of a young nymph, Daphne. As she ran, she called out to the gods for help and they turned her into a bay tree – probably not quite what she had in mind. Apollo wove himself a wreath of bay and decreed that, thereafter, all who create beauty should be rewarded with a circlet of Daphne's leaves.

Michaelmas daisies suggest a farewell, raspberries express remorse, purple verbena conveys the loving message 'I weep for you', and the circle of bay is a symbolic reward of merit.

Zinnias

Multi-coloured zinnias express 'thoughts of absent friends', the more melodramatic 'I mourn your absence' or, quite simply, 'I miss you'.

Zinnias originate in Mexico where they were known as *mal de ojos* (literally 'sick to the eye'), as Mexicans considered them to be completely devoid of beauty. They were discovered growing there by a professor of medicine called Johan Gottfried Zinn in the middle of the eighteenth century. Ignoring local opinion, he sent some as a gift to his friend the Marchioness of Bute, who was married to the British Ambassador in Madrid. The plants had barely crossed the sea when Zinn, aged only thirty-two, died unexpectedly of consumption.

His friend the Marchioness was the daughter-in-law of one John Stuart Bute, director of the Royal Botanic Gardens at Kew. Her zinnias were obviously thriving and she decided to send him some from Spain. But disaster struck again. Some time after they arrived, Bute, reaching for a rare plant growing on a cliff face, overbalanced and fell to his death.

Little wonder then that the unalluring Mexican zinnia became a floral memento of absent friends, both near and far. Today the meaning remains but zinnias have had something of a make-over. After much hybridization in the twentieth century, they have become an unexpectedly pretty way to remember friends.

Do not be put off by the zinnia's apparently homicidal past – they are charming flowers to give to friends or to have at home. Specific colours were allocated different meanings, with white symbolizing goodness, scarlet constancy and yellow daily remembrance. A mixture of colours represents thoughts of absent friends.

Zinnias are simple flowers and somehow quite contemporary. I like to arrange them massed in colourful china bowls or packed into rows of old jam-jars or small glass vases, like the one used here. They are sometimes available as flowering plants, which look very jolly in little pots marching along a dining table.
Zinnias (Zinnia elegans)

Garlands of roses, made by wiring the flowers individually and then binding them onto a fine circular frame, have long been popular headdresses for weddings. To give the symbolism wider appeal, I designed this alternative wreath of roses. It is basically a circle of similar but unmatched tumblers that have simply been filled with water and roses. *Et voilà…* an effortless wreath of roses to decorate a table for a retirement dinner or for a lunch to remember a much-missed old friend. It would look strikingly chic with roses of one variety and silver tumblers arranged in two concentric rings.

Roses (Rosa 'Evelyn', 'Tower Bridge', 'Saint Cecilia' and 'Albertine')

The delicate beauty of a garland of full-blown roses symbolizes the reward of virtue – a fragrant way to say 'you have been exemplary'.

A wreath of roses

The long history of the rose is littered with references to beauty, love and virtue. A Jewish legend relates how its colour came from the first blood shed on earth in the battle between good and evil, the virtuous dead laid to rest in fields of roses. The Romans used wreaths and garlands of roses not only to beautify their infamously debauched feasts but also to bedeck young men when they first went to war.

The Christian Church was slow to accept the rose as a holy symbol because of its decadent pagan past. But its popularity had obvious advantages and, eventually, it was incorporated into one of the alternative names for the Virgin Mary, the Rosa Mystica. When the rosary was devised as a symbolic circular garland of prayers to the Virgin, the links between the rose and righteousness increased. The flower that embodied the excesses of the dissolute Roman Empire had been clothed in the mantle of respectability, purity and goodness. Ever since, a garland of roses in poetry, songs or paintings has signified exemplary virtue.

Lathyrus

A bottle-shaped vase is ideal for this arrangement as it holds the flowers securely in place. Sweet peas are delicate flowers, so I arranged the rosemary and geraniums first to avoid bruising. You could make the message more optimistic – and hint at the possibility of meeting again – by choosing brighter sweet peas and a clear or coloured container.

On the previous page, I have arranged sweet peas on their own in a multitude of small glass phials. Repetition is an effective floral technique that can make a few stems look like a lot.

Right: Sweet peas (Lathyrus odoratus *'Juventis'),* rosemary (Rosmarinus officinalis) *and mourning widow geraniums* (Geranium phaeum)

Previous pages: Sweet peas (Lathyrus odoratus *'Bicolor', 'Deep Purple' and 'Paintbrush Lavender')*

Sweet peas, rosemary & mourning widow geraniums

Sweet peas are a complete delight: frilly, frivolous and scented, too. They were hybridized extensively during the nineteenth century to produce ever-larger flowers in a progressively shocking melange of colours. They soon became a favourite in summer gardens. The plethora of flowers produced on a stem also made them a favourite parting gift to friends and family – a neat explanation for how they might have gained their meaning in the language of flowers.

The mourning widow geranium is aptly named. Its tiny purple-black flowers might have fallen straight from a widow's bonnet. Their colour, though rich and glorious, certainly inspired their woeful symbolic meaning, which brings us neatly to remembrance and its links with rosemary. It has long been known that rosemary has a powerful effect on blood circulation. In Ancient Greece, scholars wore wreaths of rosemary on their heads to increase circulation to the brain and improve the memory.

Remembrance naturally precedes thoughts of departure and death, but we can end on a happier note. Rosemary was believed to be a gift from Aphrodite, and so it was also strongly linked to joyful aspects of life: matters of the heart, marriage, beauty and even rejuvenation.

Sweet peas denote a departure, the mourning widow geraniums
symbolize melancholy, and rosemary promises to remember.

Poppies

Communicating sentiments of
consolation, poppies symbolize oblivion to sorrow.
Red poppies have also come to represent remembrance.

Opium poppies (*Papaver somniferum*) probably originated in Greece, where the flowers were traditionally dedicated to Hypnos and Morpheus, the gods of sleep and dreams. This link with the unconscious state stems, of course, from the narcotic effects of opium, the substance produced from the poppies' milky sap. It was administered to bring relief, consolation and even oblivion to anyone suffering physically or emotionally. Its power to annihilate as well as restore was also recognized, and poppies were respectfully regarded as magical flowers.

The Romans were great poppy — and perhaps even opium — devotees. They introduced it to other countries where it brought financial consolation to the natives who grew it.

Today, it is illegal to grow opium poppies in some countries. Now, all the opium-free species, including the wild poppy (*Papaver rhoeas*), have also come to have the same association with consolation, oblivion and, in the case of white poppies, sleep — pure and simple.

Many types of poppy are now produced commercially and supplied ready-treated for longevity. You can increase the life expectancy of home-grown flowers by holding the cut stem over a candle flame for a few seconds to seal it. Try arranging poppies in narrow-necked vases so their contorted stems can be appreciated as much as their flowers. Poppies tied with rosemary (remembrance, see page 150) makes a thoughtful gift for the recently bereaved.

Poppies (Papaver somniferum 'Black Beauty')

153

glossary

Flowers and their related meanings

Acacia Concealed love; Friendship
Acanthus Fine art; Artifice
Achillea War; Cure for heartache 130
Aconite Misanthropy; Treachery
Agapanthus Love letter
Almond blossom Hope
Aloe Superstition; Grief
Amaranthus see **Love-lies-bleeding**
Amaryllis (*Amaryllis belladonna*) Beautiful but timid
  or silent
Amaryllis (*Hippeastrum*) Pride; Splendid beauty 133
American linden Matrimony
Anemone, garden (*Anemone coronaria*) Pain of
  parting; Abandonment; Love's transience 108
Anemone, Japanese (*A. x hybrida*) Desertion
  Anemone, wild (*A. blanda* or *A. nemorosa*)
  Anticipation; Expectation
Angelica Inspiration 24
Apple Temptation
Apple blossom Repentance; Preference 118
Aquilegia see **Columbine**
Ash tree Grandeur
Aspen Lamentation
Auricula Painting 53
Auricula, scarlet Avarice
Autumn leaves Melancholy
Azalea Romance; Chinese symbol of womanhood

Basil Best wishes; Good luck 20
Bay leaf 'I change but in death'
Bay wreath Reward of merit 142
Beech A lovers' tryst; Prosperity 94
Begonia Beware!
Bell flower see **Campanula**
Bells of Ireland (*Molucella laevis*) Good luck 19
Bindweed 'Let us unite' 74
Birch Graceful; Meek 133
Bird of paradise Magnificence
Bluebell Constancy; Humility; Kindness 34
Borage Bluntness; Rudeness
Box Constancy in friendship; Stoicism 53
Bramble Difficulties; Remorse; Suffering 112
Broom Humility; Neatness
Buttercup Childishness; Cheerfulness; Riches 16

Cabbage Profit
Cactus Warmth; Endurance
Calla lily Feminine Beauty; Delicacy; Modesty 78
Camellia, pink Admiration; 'Longing for you'
Camellia, red 'You are a flame in my heart';
  Unpretending excellence 85
Camellia, white Perfect loveliness; 'You are adorable'
Camomile Patience; Energy in adversity
Campanula Constancy; Gratitude 12
Campanula, small, white Gratitude 12
Canterbury bells Gratitude; Acknowledgment
Carnation clove, red 'Yes!'

Carnation, deep red Passion; Heartbreak
Carnation, general mixed colours Pride and beauty;
  Health and energy
Carnation, pink 'I will never forget you'
Carnation, purple Capricious; Whimsical
Carnation, yellow 'You have disappointed me!'
Celandine Joys to come
Cherry blossom Spiritual beauty
Chervil Sincerity
Chestnut 'Do me justice'
Christmas rose (*Helleborus niger*) Tranquillize; 'You
  relieve my anxiety'
Chrysanthemum, Chinese 'You are a great friend'
Chrysanthemum, rose-pink In love
Chrysanthemum, white Truth
Chrysanthemum, yellow Slighted love
Cinquefoil (*Potentilla*) Beloved child
Clematis Vacuous beauty; Artifice 102
Clematis, evergreen Poverty
Clematis, wild Safety; Security
Clover, four-leaved 'Be mine!'
Clover, white 'Think of me'
Cockscomb (*Celosia*) Frippery; Affectation
Columbine Caprice; Folly 56
Corn Riches
Cornflower Delicacy; Refinement
Cow parsley (Queen Anne's lace) Fantasy 70
Crab-apple blossom Ill-tempered
Cress Stability; Power

Crocus Cheerfulness; Youthful gladness

Crown imperial (*Fritillaria imperialis*) Majesty; Power; Pride 133

Cup and saucer vine (*Cobaea scandens*) Gossip

Currants, bunch of 'You please all!'

Currants, flowering 'Your frown will kill me!'

Cyclamen Diffidence; Resignation

Cypress Mourning; Death

Cypress with a marigold Despair

Daffodil Unrequited love; Chivalry

Dahlia Good taste; Elegance and stability 62

Daisy Innocence and beauty; Simplicity 37

Daisy, double Participation

Damson tree Independence

Dandelion Coquetry; Wishes come true

Daphne (*Daphne mezereum*) 'I desire to please!'

Daphne (*Daphne odora*) 'I would not have you otherwise'

Datura (thorn apple) Deceitful charms

Delphinium Airy

Dianthus Make haste

Dogwood, flowering (*Cornus*) 'I am indifferent to you'

Dragon plant (*Dracunculus*) A snare

Edelweiss Noble courage; Daring

Elder Compassion; Zealousness

Elm Dignity and grace

Eucalyptus Protection

Eucharis Maidenly charms 70

Euphorbia Hope in misery

Evening primrose Inconstancy

Everlasting pea Lasting pleasures; 'Go not away!'

Fennel Force; Strength; Worthy of praise

Fern Fascination; Sincerity 78

Feverfew Protection

Fig Longevity; Argument

Fig tree Prolific

Fir tree Time

Flytrap 'Caught at last'; Deceit 88

Forget-me-not True love; Unforgotten 108

Forsythia Anticipation; Expectation 20

Foxglove Insincerity; Self-ambition 98

Fritillary, snake's head (*Fritillaria meleagris*) Persecution; Vexation 102

Fuchsia Good taste; Humble love

Fuchsia, scarlet Taste

Gardenia Transport to ecstasy; 'I am too happy!' 72

Garlic Courage; Strength

Gentian Integrity

Geranium, ivy 'I engage you for the next dance'

Geranium, lemon Unexpected meeting

Geranium, mourning widow Melancholy 150

Geranium, oakleaf True friendship

Geranium, red Comfort 20

Geranium, rose 'I prefer you!'

Gladiolus Ready-armed

Glory lily (*Gloriosa superba*) Union of the lover and the beloved 88

Gloxinia Love at first sight

Goldenrod Encouragement

Gooseberry Anticipation 19

Grape vine Drunkenness 65

Grass Industry; Perseverance; Usefulness 24

Guelder rose (*Viburnum opulus*) Thoughts of heaven; Winter; Age 138

Harebell Grief; Retirement

Hawthorn Hope

Hazel Reconciliation

Heartsease 'Think of me'

Heather Good luck; Protection

Heliotrope 'I adore you'; Devotion

Hellebore Scandal; Calumny (see also **Christmas rose**) 94

Hemp Fate

Hibiscus Delicate beauty

Hippeastrum see **Amaryllis** (*Hippeastrum*)

Holly Domestic happiness; Strength; Defence

Hollyhock Fecundity; Fertility 23

Honesty Honesty and sincerity

Honeysuckle Devoted love; Fidelity; Fraternal love

Hops Injustice

Hornbeam Ornament

Horse chestnut Luxury

Houseleek (*Sempervivum*) Domestic economy

Hyacinths in general Constancy; Jealousy; Sport

Hyacinth, blue Constancy

Hyacinth, purple Sorrow; 'Please forgive me'

Hyacinth, white Beauty and constancy 121

Hydrangea Heartlessness; Boastfulness; Vanity; Frigidity 96

Iris Good news; A message 14

Ivy Constancy; Marriage

Ivy leaf Friendship

Ivy trail Marriage

Jacob's ladder 'Come down to me!'

Jasmine, white Amiability; Friendliness 58

Jasmine, yellow Grace and elegance

Jonquil 'I desire a return of affection'

Judas tree (*Cercis*) Betrayal

Juniper Protection; Succour

Kingcup (marsh marigold) Desire for riches

Laburnum Pensive beauty

Larch Audacity; Boldness 65

Larkspur Levity; Hilarity

Larkspur, purple Haughtiness

Laurel, wreath of Glory

Lauristinus (*Viburnum tinus*) 'I die if neglected'

Lavatera Sweet disposition

Lavender Distrust; Defiance

Lemon Zest

Lemon blossom Discretion; Fidelity in love

Lettuce Cold-hearted

Lichen Dejection; Solitude 118

Lilac, purple First love; First emotions of love 44

Lilac, white Memories of youth and youthful innocence 141

Lily-of-the-valley Return of happiness 121

Lily, orange Hatred

Lily, white Purity; Innocence 30

Lily, yellow Gaiety; Falsehood

Linden leaf (*Tilia*) Marriage

Linden tree or sprig (*Tilia*) Conjugal happiness

Livingstone daisy (*Mesembryanthemum*) 'Your looks freeze me'

Lobelia Malevolence

Locust tree Love beyond the grave

Lotus flower Estranged love

Lotus plant Eloquence

Love-in-a-mist see **Nigella**

Love-lies-bleeding (*Amaranthus*) Hopeless but not heartless 86

Lupin Dejection; Imagination

Lychnis Religious enthusiasm.

Magnolia Love of nature; Nobility

Magnolia grandiflora Peerless and proud 133

Maidenhair fern Discretion; Secret love

Mallow (*Malva moschata*) Good, sweet and kind

Maple Reserve

Marigold, African (*Tagetes erecta*) Vulgarity

Marigold, French (*Tagetes patula*) Jealousy

Marigold, garden Grief; Unease

Marjoram Blushes; Happiness 65

Meadowsweet Usefulness

Michaelmas daisy Afterthought; Farewell 142

Mignonette 'Your qualities surpass your charms'

Mimosa Sensitivity; Modesty

Mint Virtue (see also **Peppermint** and **Spearmint**)

Mistletoe 'I surmount all obstacles'

Mock orange (*Philadelphus*) Counterfeit

Monkshood (*Aconitum*) Beware… a foe is near

Morning glory (*Ipomoea*) Affectation; Coquette

Moss Maternal love 12
Mulberry, black 'I will not survive you'
Mulberry, white Wisdom
Mullein (*Verbascum*) Good-natured
Mushroom Suspicion
Myrtle Love; Symbol of marriage 122

Narcissus Egotism; Vanity; Self-love 111
Nasturtium Patriotism; Victory in war
Nettle Cruelty; Slander 112
Nigella 'You puzzle me'; Perplexity

Oak Strength; Courage 62
Oak leaf Bravery and humanity 62
Oak sprig Hospitality 62
Oats Soul of music; Musical 130
Oleander Beware
Olive Peace; Wisdom
Orange blossom Purity equal to loveliness
Orange tree Generosity; Virginity
Orchid A belle; Beauty
Orchid, butterfly (*Phalaenopsis*) Gaiety
Orchid, cattleya Mature charms 125
Orchid, slipper Capricious beauty 101
Oregano Birth 19

Palm Victory and success
Pansy 'Think of me' 54
Parsley Lasting pleasures; Festivity 138
Pasque flower (*Pulsatilla*) Unpretentious; 'You have
    no claims'
Passionflower Faith; Spirituality 138
Peach 'Your charms are unequalled'
Peach blossom 'I am your captive'
Pear Affection 58
Pear tree Comfort
Peony Bashfulness; Shame; Devotion 40
Peppermint Cordiality; Warmth 62
Periwinkle, blue Sweet memories of early friendship
    65
Petunia Resentment; Anger
Phlox Unanimity 122
Pine (spruce) Farewell; Hope
Pineapple 'You are perfect'
Pink, garden, red (*Dianthus*) Pure and ardent love
Pink, variegated Refusal
Pink, white 'You are fair'; Talented
Plum tree Fidelity; 'Keep your promise!'
Poinsettia 'Be of good cheer'
Polyanthus Pride of riches; Confidence
Pomegranate Foolishness; Conceit; Pride
Poplar, black Courage
Poppy Consolation; Death; Oblivion to sorrow 153

Poppy, red Remembrance
Poppy, white Sleep
Primrose Early youth; Young love; Modesty 44
Primula Diffidence
Privet Prohibition
Pulmonaria 'You are my life'
Pumpkin Coarseness; Greed

Quaking grass Agitation
Queen Anne's lace see Cow parsley
Quince Temptation

Ranunculus Dazzling; 'You are radiant with charms';
    'You are rich in attractions' 50
Raspberry Remorse 142
Reeds Music
Rhododendron Beware!; Danger 61
Rhubarb Advice 61
Rocket Rivalry
Rose, blood-red, open 'I love you' 80–1
Rose, briar 'I wound to heal'
Rose, Burgundy Unconscious beauty
Rose, cabbage Love's ambassador 80–1
Rose, China Beauty always new
Rose, damask Freshness; Brilliant complexion
Rose, dog Pleasure and pain
Rose, eglantine Poetry
Rose, full-blown 'You are beautiful' 80–1
Rose, full-blown, placed over two buds Secrecy 80–1
Rose, Japanese or rugosa 'Beauty is your only
    attraction' 98
Rose leaf 'You may hope'
Rose, moss Voluptuous; Superior merits!
Rose, moss, in bud Confessed love
Rose, multiflora Grace 82
Rose, musk Capricious beauty 80–1
Rose, pink Perfect happiness 126
Rose, pink, in bud New Love
Rose, red, in bud Young, pure and lovely 33
Rose, striped Variety 80–1
Rose, tea 'I'll always remember'
Rose, white, dried Death before loss of innocence
Rose, white, in bud Innocent of love; Girlhood 37
Rose, white, open 'I am worthy of you' 80–1
Rose, white, withered Transient impressions
Rose, wild or single Simplicity; 'I still love you'
Rose, yellow Infidelity; Jealousy; Decrease of love
Roses in general Beauty and love 82
Roses, bouquet of full-blown Gratitude
Roses, red and white together Unity 80–1
Roses, wreath of full-blown The reward of virtue 146
Rosemary Remembrance; Fidelity; Commitment 150
Rushes (*Juncus effusus*) Calm and docility 130

Sage Health; Long life 19
St John's Wort (*Hypericum*) Superstition; Animosity
Scabious Unfortunate love; Widowhood
Scabious, purple Mourning
Scot's thistle Retaliation
Shamrock Lightheartedness 16
Silverleaf (*Potentilla anserina*) Naivety 34
Smilax Loveliness
Snapdragon Presumption; 'No, never!'
Snowdrop Consolation and hope
Spearmint Warmth inside
Solomon's seal Permanence; Healing 121
Sorrel (*Oxalis*) Parental affection
Speedwell (*Veronica*) Female fidelity
Spindle tree 'Your image is engraved on my heart'
Star of Bethlehem (*Ornithogalum*) Reconciliation;
    Purity; Guidance
Stephanotis 'Come to me!'; Happy marriage; Desire
    to travel 72
Stock Lasting beauty; Contented life 129
Stonecrop (*Sedum*) Tranquillity
Strawberry Perfect goodness 33
Sunflower, dwarf 'Your devout admirer'; Adoration
Sunflower, tall Pride; Haughtiness
Sweet pea Departure; A meeting; Delicate pleasures;
    'Thanks for a lovely time' 150
Sweet William Willing to please; Gallant 33

Thistle Austerity
Thyme Strength and courage 19
Trillium grandiflorum Enthusiasm
Trillium pictum Modest beauty
Tuberose Dangerous pleasures 112
Tulips in general Fame and renown 86, 94
Tulip, red Declaration of love 86
Tulip, striped 'You have beautiful eyes' 86
Tulip, yellow Hopeless love 86

Venus Flytrap see Flytrap
Verbascum see Mullein
Verbena Sensibility
Verbena, pink Family union
Verbena, purple Regret; 'I weep for you' 142
Verbena, white 'Pray for me'
Veronica see Speedwell
Vetch 'I cling to you'
Viola, blue 'I will always be true and loyal' 54
Viola, purple 'You are in my thoughts' 54
Viola, white Modesty; Purity; 'Let's take a chance on
    happiness!' 54
Viola, yellow Rural happiness 54
Violet, Sweet (*Viola odorata*) Modesty; Decency;
    Innocence 43

Wallflower Fidelity in adversity 101

Water lily Great beauty with coldness of heart; Purity 107

Wax plant (*Hoya*) Sculpture

Weeping willow Melancholy

Wheat Wealth and prosperity

Willow herb Pretension

Winter cherry Deception

Wisteria 'I cling to you'; Mutual trust

Witch hazel (*Hamamelis*) 'A spell is on me!'

Yew Sorrow; Penitence

Zinnia, multi-coloured Thoughts of absent friends; 'I mourn your absence'; 'I miss you' 145

Zinnia, scarlet Constancy

Zinnia, white Goodness

Zinnia, yellow Daily remembrance

Meanings and their related flowers

'A spell is on me' Witch hazel (*Hamamelis*)

Abandonment Garden anemone (*Anemone coronaria*) 108

Acknowledgment Canterbury bells

Admiration Pink camellia

Adoration Dwarf sunflower

Advice Rhubarb 61

Affectation Cockscomb (*Celosia*); Morning glory (*Ipomaea*)

Affection Pear 58

Afterthought Michaelmas daisy 142

Age Guelder rose (*Viburnum opulus*) 138

Agitation Quaking grass

Airy Delphinium

Amiability White jasmine 58

Anger Petunia

Animosity St John's wort (*Hypericum*)

Anticipation Forsythia 20; Wild anemone (*Anemone blanda* or *A. nemorosa*); Gooseberry 19

Argument Fig

Artifice Acanthus; Clematis 102

Audacity Larch 65

Austerity Thistle

Avarice Scarlet auricula

Bashfulness Peony 40

'Be of good cheer' Poinsettia

Beautiful but timid or silent Amaryllis (*Amaryllis belladonna*)

Beauty Orchid

Beauty always new China rose

Beauty and constancy White hyacinth 121

Beauty and love Roses in general

'Beauty is your only attraction' Japanese or rugosa rose 98

Belle Orchid

Beloved child Cinquefoil (*Potentilla*)

'Be mine!' Four-leaved clover

Best wishes Basil 20

Betrayal Judas tree (*Cercis*)

Beware! Begonia; Oleander; Rhododendron 61

Beware... a foe is near Monkshood (*Aconitum*)

Birth Oregano 19

Bluntness Borage

Blushes Marjoram 65

Boastfulness Hydrangea 96

Boldness Larch 65

Bravery and humanity Oak leaf 62

Calm and docility Rushes (*Juncus effusus*) 130

Calumny Hellebore 94

Caprice Columbine 56

Capricious Purple carnation

Capricious beauty Slipper orchid 101; Musk rose 80–1

'Caught at last!' Flytrap 88

Cheerfulness Buttercup 16

Childishness Buttercup 16

Chivalry Daffodil

Coarseness Pumpkin

Cold-hearted Lettuce

'Come down to me!' Jacob's ladder

'Come to me!' Stephanotis 72

Comfort Red geranium 20; Pear tree

Commitment Rosemary 150

Compassion Elder

Concealed love Acacia

Conceit Pomegranate

Confessed love Moss rosebud

Confidence Polyanthus

Conjugal happiness Linden (*Tilia*) tree or sprig

Consolation Poppy 153

Consolation and hope Snowdrop

Constancy Bluebell 34; Blue hyacinth and hyacinths in general; Ivy; Scarlet zinnia

Constancy in friendship Box 53

Contented life Stock 129

Coquetry Dandelion

Coquette Morning glory (*Ipomaea*)

Cordiality Peppermint 62

Counterfeit Mock orange (*Philadelphus*)

Courage Garlic; Oak 62; Black poplar

Cruelty Nettle 112

Cure for heartache Achillea 130

Daily remembrance Yellow zinnia

Danger Rhododendron 61

Dangerous pleasures Tuberose 112

Daring Edelweiss

Dazzling Ranunculus 50

Death Cypress; Poppy 153

Death before loss of innocence Dried white roses

Deceit Flytrap 88

Deceitful charms Thorn apple (*Datura*)

Decency Sweet violet (*Viola odorata*) 43

Deception Winter cherry

Declaration of love Red tulip 86

Decrease of love Yellow rose

Defence Holly

Defiance Lavender

Dejection Lichen 118; Lupin

Delicacy Calla lily 78

Delicate beauty Hibiscus

Delicate pleasures Sweet pea 150

Departure Sweet pea 150

Desire for riches Kingcup (marsh marigold)

Desire to travel Stephanotis 72

Despair Cypress with a marigold

Desertion Japanese anemone (*Anemone × hybrida*)

Devoted love Honeysuckle

Devotion Heliotrope; Peony 40

Difficulties Bramble 112

Diffidence Cyclamen; Primula

Dignity and grace Elm

Discretion Lemon blossom; Maidenhair fern

Distrust Lavender

'Do me justice' Chestnut

Domestic economy Houseleek (*Sempervivum*)

Domestic happiness Holly

Drunkenness Grape vine 65

Early youth Primrose 44

Egotism Narcissus 111

Elegance and stability Dahlia 62

Eloquence Lotus plant

Encouragement Goldenrod

Endurance Cactus

Energy in adversity Camomile

Enthusiasm *Trillium grandiflorum*

Estranged love Lotus flower

Expectation Wild anemone (*Anemone blanda* or *A. nemorosa*); Forsythia 20

Faith Passionflower 138

Falsehood Yellow lily

Fame and renown Tulips in general 86, 94

Family union Pink verbena

Fantasy Cow parsley (Queen Anne's lace) 70

Farewell Michaelmas daisy 142; Pine (spruce)
Fascination Fern 78
Fate Hemp
Fecundity Hollyhock 23
Female fidelity Speedwell (*Veronica*)
Feminine beauty Calla lily 78
Fertility Hollyhock 23
Festivity Parsley 138
Fidelity Honeysuckle; Plum tree; Rosemary 150
Fidelity in adversity Wallflower 101
Fidelity in love Lemon blossom
Fine art Acanthus
First emotions of love Purple lilac 44
First love Purple lilac 44
Folly Columbine 56
Foolishness Pomegranate
Force Fennel
Fraternal love Honeysuckle
Freshness Damask rose
Friendship Acacia; Ivy leaf
Frigidity Hydrangea 96
Frippery Cockscomb (*Celosia*)

Gaiety Yellow lily; Butterfly orchid (*Phalaenopsis*)
Gallant Sweet William 33
Generosity Orange tree
Girlhood White rosebud 37
Glory Wreath of laurel
'Go not away!' Everlasting pea
Good luck Basil 20; Bells of Ireland (*Molucella laevis*) 19; Heather
Good-natured Mullein (*Verbascum*)
Goodness White zinnia
Good news Iris 14
Good, sweet and kind Mallow (*Malva moschata*)
Good taste Dahlia 62; Fuchsia
Gossip Cup and saucer vine (*Cobaea scandens*)
Grace Multiflora rose 82
Grace and elegance Yellow jasmine
Graceful Birch 133
Grandeur Ash tree
Gratitude Campanula (small, white) 12; Canterbury bells; Bouquet of full-blown roses
Great beauty with coldness of heart Water lily 107
Greed Pumpkin
Grief Aloe; Harebell; Garden marigold
Guidance Star of Bethlehem (*Ornithogalum*)

Happiness Marjoram 65
Happy marriage Stephanotis 72
Hatred Orange lily
Haughtiness Purple larkspur; Tall sunflower
Healing Solomon's seal 121

Health Sage 19
Health and energy Mixed colour carnations
Heartbreak Deep red carnation
Heartlessness Hydrangea 96
Hilarity Larkspur
Honesty and sincerity Honesty
Hope Almond blossom; Hawthorn; Pine (spruce)
Hope in misery Euphorbia
Hopeless but not heartless Love-lies-bleeding (*Amaranthus*) 86
Hopeless love Yellow tulip 86
Hospitality Oak sprig 62
Humble love Fuchsia
Humility Bluebell 34; Broom

'I adore you' Heliotrope
'I am indifferent to you' Flowering dogwood (*Cornus*)
'I am too happy!' Gardenia 72
'I am worthy of you' Open white rose 80–1
'I am your captive' Peach blossom
'I change but in death' Bay leaf
'I cling to you' Vetch; Wisteria
'I desire a return of affection' Jonquil
'I desire to please' Daphne (*Daphne mezereum*)
'I die if neglected' Lauristinus (*Viburnum tinus*)
'I engage you for the next dance' Ivy geranium
'I'll always remember' Tea rose
'I love' Red chrysanthemum
'I love you' Open blood-red rose 80–1
'I miss you' Multi-coloured zinnias 145
'I mourn your absence' Multi-coloured zinnias 145
'I prefer you!' Rose geranium
'I still love you' Wild rose or single rose
'I surmount all obstacles' Mistletoe
'I weep for you' Purple verbena 142
'I will always be true' Blue viola 54
'I will never forget you' Pink carnation
'I will not survive you' Black mulberry
'I would not have you otherwise' Daphne (*Daphne odora*)
'I wound to heal' Briar rose
Ill-tempered Crab-apple blossom
Imagination Lupin
Inconstancy Evening primrose
Independence Damson tree
Indiscretion Almond tree
Industry Grass 24
Infidelity Yellow rose
Injustice Hops
In love Rose-pink chrysanthemum
Innocence Sweet violet (*Viola odorata*) 43; White lily 30
Innocence and beauty Daisy 37

Innocent of love White rosebud 37
Insincerity Foxglove 98
Inspiration Angelica 24
Integrity Gentian

Jealousy Hyacinth; French marigold (*Tagetes patula*); Yellow rose
Joys to come Celandine

Kindness Bluebell 34
'Keep your promise!' Plum tree

Lamentation Aspen
Lasting beauty Stock 129
Lasting pleasures Everlasting pea; Parsley 138
'Let's take a chance on happiness!' White viola 54
'Let us unite' Bindweed 74
Levity Larkspur
Lightheartedness Shamrock 16
Longevity Fig
'Longing for you' Pink camellia
Long life Sage 19
Love Myrtle 122
Love at first sight Gloxinia
Love beyond the grave Locust tree
Love letter Agapanthus
Love of nature Magnolia
Loveliness Smilax
Lovers' tryst Beech 94
Love's ambassador Cabbage rose 80–1
Love's transience Garden anemone (*Anemone coronaria*) 108
Luxury Horse chestnut

Magnificence Bird of paradise
Maidenly charms Eucharis 70
Majesty Crown imperial (*Fritillaria imperialis*) 133
'Make haste!' Dianthus
Malevolence Lobelia
Marriage Ivy or trail of ivy; Linden (*Tilia*) leaf
Marriage, symbol of Myrtle 122
Maternal love Moss 12
Matrimony American linden
Mature charms Cattleya orchid 125
Meek Birch 133
Meeting Sweet pea 150
Melancholy Autumn leaves; Mourning widow geranium 150; Weeping willow
Memories of youth and youthful innocence White lilac 141
Message Iris 14
Misanthropy Aconite
Modest beauty *Trillium pictum*

Modesty Calla lily 78; Mimosa; Primrose 44; Sweet violet (*Viola odorata*) 43; White viola 54
Mourning Cypress; Purple scabious
Music Reeds
Musical Oats 130
Mutual trust Wisteria
'My best days are over' Autumn crocus (*Colchicum autumnale*)

Naivety Silverleaf (*Potentilla*) 34
Neatness Broom
New love Pink rosebud
Nobility Magnolia
Noble courage Edelweiss
'No, never!' Snapdragon

Oblivion to sorrow Poppy 153
Ornament Hornbeam
'Our hearts and souls are united' Phlox 122

Pain of parting Garden anemone (*Anemone coronaria*) 108
Painting Auricula 53
Parental affection Sorrel (*Oxalis*)
Participation Double daisy
Passion Deep red carnation
Patience Camomile
Patriotism Nasturtium
Peace Olive
Peerless and proud *Magnolia grandiflora* 133
Penitence Yew
Pensive beauty Laburnum
Perfect goodness Strawberry 33
Perfect happiness Pink rose 126
Perfect loveliness White camellia
Permanence Solomon's seal 121
Persecution Snake's head fritillary (*Fritillaria meleagris*) 102
Perseverance Grass 24
'Please forgive me' Purple hyacinth
Pleasure and pain Dog rose
Poetry Eglantine rose
Power Cress; Crown imperial (*Fritillaria imperialis*) 133
'Pray for me' White verbena
Preference Apple blossom 118
Presumption Snapdragon
Pretension Willow herb
Pride Amaryllis (*Hippeastrum*) 133; Crown imperial (*Fritillaria imperialis*) 133; Pomegranate; Tall sunflower
Pride and beauty Mixed colour carnations
Pride of riches Polyanthus

Profit Cabbage
Prohibition Privet
Prolific Fig tree
Prosperity Beech 94
Protection Eucalyptus; Feverfew; Heather; Juniper
Pure and ardent love Red garden pink (*Dianthus*)
Purity Star of Bethlehem (*Ornithogalum*); Water lily 107; White lily 30; White viola 54
Purity equal to loveliness Orange blossom

Ready-armed Gladiolus
Reconciliation Hazel; Star of Bethlehem (*Ornithogalum*)
Refinement Cornflower
Refusal Striped carnation; Variegated garden pink
Regret Purple verbena 142
Religious enthusiasm Lychnis
Remembrance Red poppy; Rosemary 150
Remorse Bramble 112; Raspberry 142
Repentance Apple blossom 118
Resentment Petunia
Resignation Cyclamen
Retaliation Scot's thistle
Retirement Harebell
Return of happiness Lily-of-the-valley 121
Reserve Maple
Reward of merit Bay wreath 142
Reward of virtue Wreath of full-blown roses 146
Riches Buttercup 16; Corn
Rivalry Rocket
Romance Azalea
Rudeness Borage
Rural happiness Yellow viola 54

Scandal Hellebore 94
Sculpture Wax plant (*Hoya*)
Secrecy Full-blown rose over two buds 80–1
Secret love Maidenhair fern
Security Wild clematis
Self-ambition Foxglove 98
Self-love Narcissus 111
Sensibility Verbena
Sensitivity Mimosa
Severity Thorns in general
Shame Peony 40
Simplicity Daisy 37; Wild rose or single rose
Sincerity Chervil; Fern 78
Slander Nettle 112
Sleep White poppy
Slighted love Yellow chrysanthemum
Snare Dragon plant (*Dracunculus*)
Solitude Lichen 118
Sorrow Purple hyacinth; Yew

Soul of music Oats 130
Spiritual beauty Cherry blossom
Spirituality Passionflower 138
Splendid beauty Amaryllis (*Hippeastrum*) 133
Sport Hyacinth
Stability Cress
Stoicism Box 53
Strength Fennel; Garlic; Holly; Oak 62
Strength and courage Thyme 19
Succour Juniper
Suffering Bramble 112
Superior merits Moss rose
Superstition Aloe; St John's wort (*Hypericum*)
Suspicion Mushroom
Sweet disposition Lavatera
Sweet memories of early friendship Blue periwinkle 65

Talented White garden pink (*Dianthus*)
Taste Scarlet fuchsia
Temptation Apple; Quince
'Thanks for a lovely time' Sweet pea 150
'Think of me' White clover; Heartsease; Pansy 54
Thoughts of absent friends Multi-coloured zinnias 145
Thoughts of heaven Guelder rose (*Viburnum opulus*) 138
Time Fir tree
Tranquillity Stonecrop (*Sedum*)
Tranquillize Christmas rose (*Helleborus niger*)
Transient impressions Withered white rose
Transport to ecstacy Gardenia 72
Treachery Aconite
True friendship Oakleaf geranium
True love Forget-me-not 108
Truth White chrysanthemum

Unanimity Phlox 122
Unconscious beauty Burgundy rose
Unease Garden marigold
Unexpected meeting Lemon geranium
Union of the lover and the beloved Glory lily (*Gloriosa superba*) 88
Unity Red and white roses together 80–1
Unpretending excellence Red camellia 85
Unpretentiousness Pasque flower (*Pulsatilla*)
Unforgotten Forget-me-not 108
Unfortunate love Scabious
Unrequited love Daffodil
Usefulness Grass 24; Meadowsweet

Vanity Hydrangea 96; Narcissus 111
Vacuous beauty Clematis 102
Vexation Snake's head fritillary (*Fritillaria meleagris*) 102

Victory and success Palm
Victory in war Nasturtium
Virginity Orange tree
Virtue Mint
Voluptuous Moss rose
Vulgar; vulgar minds African marigold (*Tagetes erecta*)

War Achillea 130
Warmth Cactus; Peppermint 62
Warmth inside Spearmint
Wealth and prosperity Wheat
Whimsical Purple carnation
Widowhood Scabious
Willing to please Sweet William 33
Winter Guelder rose (*Viburnum opulus*) 138
Wisdom White mulberry; Olive
Wishes come true Dandelion
Womanhood, Chinese symbol of Azalea
Woman's good luck gift White carnation
Worthy of praise Fennel

'Yes!' Red clove carnation
'You are adorable' White camellia
'You are a flame in my heart' Red camellia 85
'You are a wonderful friend' Chinese
chrysanthemum
'You are beautiful' Full-blown rose 80–1
'You are fair' White garden pink (*Dianthus*)
'You are in my thoughts' Purple viola 54
'You are my life' Pulmonaria
'You are perfect' Pineapple
'You are radiant with charms' Ranunculus 50
'You are rich in attractions' Ranunculus 50
'You have beautiful eyes' Tulip (striped) 86
'You have no claims' Pasque flower (*Pulsatilla*)
'You may hope' Rose leaf
'You please all!' Bunch of currants
'You puzzle me' Nigella (Love-in-a-mist)
'You relieve my anxiety' Christmas rose (*Helleborus niger*)
Young love Primrose 44
Young, pure and lovely Red rosebud 33
'Your charms are unequalled' Peach
'Your devout admirer' Dwarf sunflower
'Your frown will kill me!' Flowering currant
'Your image is engraved on my heart' Spindle tree
'Your looks freeze me' Livingstone daisy (*Mesembryanthemum*)
'Your qualities surpass your charms' Mignonette
Youthful gladness Crocus

Zealousness Elder
Zest Lemon

bibliography

Kristyna Arcati, *The Language of Flowers: a beginner's guide* (Hodder & Stoughton Headway, 1997)
David Austin, *English Roses* (Conran Octopus, 1996)
David Austin, Shrub Roses and Climbing Roses (Antique Collectors Club, 1994)
Maggie Campbell-Culver, *The Origin of Plants* (Headline, 2001)
Arthur Cotterell, *Classical Mythology* (Anness, 2000)
JG Frazer, *The Golden Bough* (Papermac, 1922)
John Gerard, *Gerards Herbal* (Senate, 1998)
Robert Graves, *Greek Myths* (Penguin Books, 1981)
Kate Greenaway, *The Language of Flowers* (Routledge, 1884)
Marina Heilmeyer, *The Language of Flowers: symbols and myths* (Prestel Verlag, 2001)
Debra N.Mancroft, *Flora Symbolica: flowers in pre-Raphaelite art* (Prestel, 2003)
Richard Mabey, *Flora Brittanica* (Sinclair-Stevenson, 1996)
Paolo Mantegazza, *The Legends of Flowers* (T. Werner Laurie, 1930)
John Marr, *An Explanation of Some Plant Names and their Identities in India* (Royal Asiatic Society, 1972)
John Parkinson, *Garden of Pleasant Flowers* (Dover, 1629)
Jane Paterson, *Flower Lore* (McCaw, Stevenson & Orr, 1870)
The RHS Encyclopedia of Plants and Flowers (Dorling Kindersley, 1992)
Sharman Apt Russell, *Anatomy of a Rose* (Arrow Books, 2002)
Marthe Seguin-Fontes, *The Language of Flowers* (Sterling, 2001)
Miranda Seymour, *A Brief History of Thyme* (John Murray, 2002)
Eleanor Sinclair-Rohde, *The Scented Garden* (Medici Society, 1989)
Eleanour Sinclair Rohde, *Shakespeare's Wild Flowers* (The Medici Society, 1935)
Pamela Todd, *Forget-me-not: a floral treasury* (Little, Brown USA, 1993)
Robert Tyas, *The Language of Flowers or Floral Emblems* (George Routledge and Son, 1869)
Robert Upstone, *The Pre-Raphaelite Dream* (Tate Publishing, 2003)
Roy Vickery, *Oxford Dictionary of Plant-Lore* (Oxford University Press, 1995)
Diana Wells, *101 Flowers and How they Got Their Names*
The resources of the Linley library

acknowledgments

This book was very much a team effort and I owe huge bunches of Campanulas and Canterbury bells to many, many people. Firstly and most importantly to my friend Jan Baldwin, who sees flowers like a medieval visionary and captures them on film with all their exquisite individuality. This book is as much hers as it is mine; to Megan Smith who expertly art directed and kept us all on course (and on earth) and whose sensitive layouts make the book a joy to look at; to the wonderful Lesley Dilcock, who added her exquisite quirky touch to every picture and her humour to every shoot, At Conran Octopus I would send bouquets of full-blown roses to my editor Katey Day, who managed to combine enthusiasm, patience and sweet calm throughout and most especially during the final writing process; to Chi Lam who took over from my dear friend Leslie Harrington and added so much inspiration; to Lorraine Dickey for thinking it would all work in the first place; and to Belinda Harley for encouraging, advising and managing. What would it be without the flowers? A few large pineapples to Covent Garden Flower Market for Dennis Edwards at Austins, who was particularly helpful with the naming of flowers; Allan and Stella at Alagar; Charlie Gardiner at Rimark; David Gorton at Bacons; Grant one and two at C.Best; and the boys at Donovan Brothers; E.E.S; Quality plants; L.Mills; Arnott and Mason; and Norman Cole. I could not have done this without the help of my wonderful team who kept things going and supported me throughout. I would send Box, Jasmine and lots of Pears to Louise Avery, Mark Lovegrove, Sam Robb, Isabelle van Lennep; Miharu Davis, Steven Riley; John Cowan, Kurt Collet and honorary life members Tracey Elson and Sharon Melehi. More full blown roses go to my initial floral inspiration, my mother and Michael Goulding (OBE) Elizabeth Baker (MBE) and Caroline Evans-Feinnes for nurturing it; and to my father-in-law Robin Denniston for all his good advice and my sister-in-law, Dr Sue Everitt, for help with homeopathic links. Finally, to my darling patient wife, a single pink rose.

The publishers would like to thank Barbara Stewart at Surfaces, Unit 1, 51 Calthrop Street, London, WC1X 0HH; and The General Trading Company, 2 Symons Street, Sloane Square, London, SW3 2TJ for the loan of the Jonathon Adler vases on pages 1 and 80–81. The fabric on the jacket is by Lee Jofa, whilst that on pages 26–28 is by Marimekko.

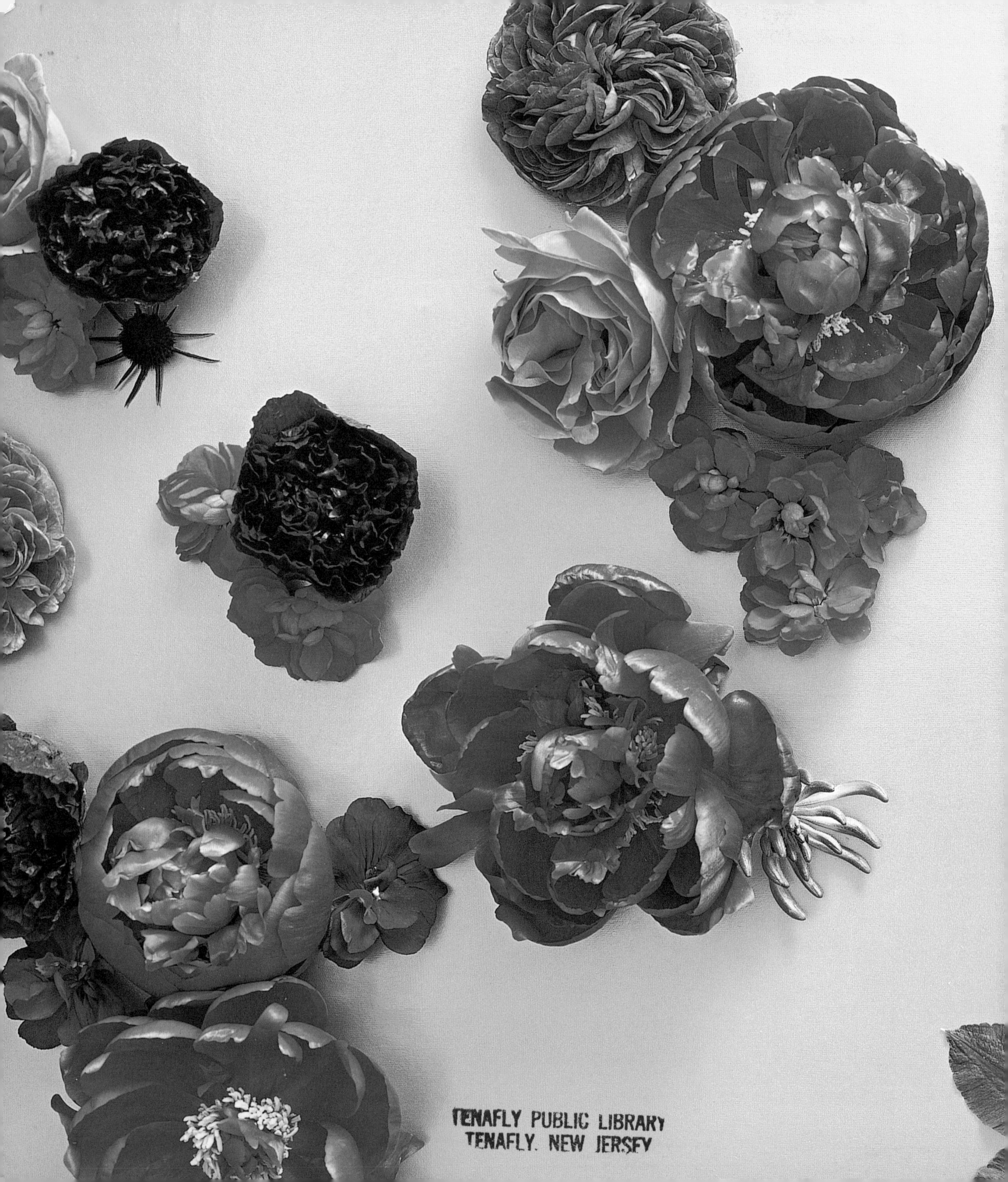